This is a work of fiction. Names, characters, places, and incidents either are the product of the author's imagination or are used fictitiously. Any resemblance to actual events or locales or persons, living or dead, is entirely coincidental.

I0107743

Side Chic 4

(Forever Ratchet)

By

La'Tonya West

Prologue- Lala

It feels like no matter what I do or how hard I try I can't get this shit right for nothing. I left Boykins and Tre behind and tried to move on because I felt in my heart it was the right thing to do. I felt like as a woman I deserved more than what he was willing to give. Hell, I'd tried everything to get him to see my love for him and realize that what we had was deeper than sex or some side affair but it didn't work. I called myself moving on to someone who knew what he wanted and wasn't about the games and bullshit only to find out that this nigga was never here for me. He'd been preying on me from day one! Pretending to care about me and my kids. I should've known something was wrong when he continued to hang around even when I wasn't answering his calls. He was what people would call "too good to be true" but I just couldn't see that shit. All I saw was how nice, kind and understanding he was. It never once crossed my mind that he could be capable of some shit like he did to Lola. As a mother that is some hard shit to digest. I feel like this was my fault! How could I have put my daughter in a situation like that? Why would I leave my babies with him? The more that I think about it the more upset I become with myself. I wonder if this was the only time that he's touched one of them. What about all of the nights that he's spent in my home? I suddenly feel sick to my stomach!

When I'd called Tre to tell him what happened. I could barely get the words out of my mouth. I really didn't want to tell him that I'd been so careless and stupid but I knew that I had to.

"Tre, I am so sorry." I'd cried when he answered the phone. "I swear I didn't mean for this to happen. I'm so sorry."

"Lala what's wrong? What are you talking about?" He'd questioned. I could hear the fear and concern in his tone. I could only imagine how fast his mind must've been racing wondering what was wrong now, never once

4

thinking something like what I was about to tell him. "Are

the babies alright? Stop crying and talk to me! What's

going on?"

"That sick motherfucka touched Lola!" I sobbed

loudly into the phone.

"What sick motherfucka? Who touched Lola? What

do you mean?" He asked question after question.

"Reggie. I'd left them with him so that I could go to

the grocery store..." I explained. "I'd left my pocketbook so

I had to turn around and come back to the house. I used

my key to let myself in and that's when I saw him on the

sofa..." I paused for a second because it felt like my words

were caught in my throat. I swallowed hard trying to

remove the large lump that had seemed to form in my

throat. "He was...touching her...touching her down

there...in her private area." I finally managed to reveal.

"What? What in the fuck do you mean, touching her

in her private area?" He roared. "Where's that nigga at

now?"

"He-he's...in the house...lying on the floor. I think I may have killed him. When I saw him touching Lola, I lost it and hit him in the head with a candleholder."

"He'd better hope like hell you did because if he's not dead when I get there, he will be."

"How could he do something like that to my baby, Tre? Why would he do that? Tre, I'm so sorry. I shouldn't have left her." After he didn't reply, I'd taken the phone from my ear and noticed that my screensaver was showing on the front of my phone...he'd hung up. I wasn't sure how to take him hanging up but I assumed that he did it because he blamed me for what had happened and he had every right to.

Now as I sit inside of this officer's car answering question after question about what happened, the only question that keeps running through my mind is...I wonder if I killed that sorry motherfucka? And to be completely honest, I'm praying that I did.

I kept my eyes fixed on my front door waiting to see if the paramedics were going to bring Reggie out on a stretcher or if he was going to walk out. All I knew was that if he walked out it was going to take every officer that was present at the scene to keep me from killing that motherfucka and no that wasn't some angry thought. That was some real shit!

"Ms. Chambers, did you hear me?" Officer Donaldson asked me from the driver's seat. He was a black man and looked to be in his early thirties. He had cocoa brown skin, dark mysterious brown eyes that damn near looked black, with a thick black mustache just above his top lip and a bald head.

I tore my eyes away from the house to look over at him. I knew that I must've look like some deranged crazy woman with my hair all over my head and my eyes puffy and red. "No sir, I didn't." I admitted truthfully. My nose was running and I used my hand to wipe it.

Officer Donaldson noticed it and reached for the box of Kleenex that sat on his dashboard and handed them to me. "Use as many as you'd like." He offered a sympathetic smile.

I took the box from his and snatched a few tissues from the box and cleaned my nose. "Thank you."

"You're welcome." He replied. "Now if you don't mind could you please answer my question?"

"Do mind repeating the question?" I looked back up at my front door.

"I asked, how long have you have known Mr. Wade?"

"I've known him for eleven months." I answered him thinking back to how I'd first met Reggie's no good ass on the day that I'd gone into labor with the girls.

"And how did the two of you meet?"

I glanced over at him again. "I was on my way back home from Boykins, VA, that's where I am originally from. I was pregnant then. I started to feel sharp pains in the bottom of my stomach, back and even my private area and so I pulled off the road at a gas station, which just so happen to be the gas station that he worked at. He must've seen me through the window in the store because he came outside to my car and asked if everything was okay. I informed him that I was pregnant and may be in labor. He called 911 for me and then went with me to the hospital. While I was in the hospital, he came to visit me. He said that he wanted to be sure that my daughters and I were okay. I thought that was very nice of him. You don't find a lot of people who will take the time out to check on a person they don't know and genuinely be concerned but Reggie was different, at least I thought he was. During the time that I was in the hospital the two of us started a friendship and exchanged numbers. He lives in South Boston, VA. So I didn't see him that much after I was released from the hospital but we talked on the phone a lot and became pretty good friends. During the time that we were friends he visited a few times. Three months ago, we began dating. He's been coming here spending the night every now and again. We had a pretty good relationship. He's always been so nice and respectful...until today." I paused and looked back up at my front door just in time to see two paramedics and an officer leading Reggie outside. He had blood on his face and all over his shirt. I noticed that he was in handcuffs.

I heard Officer Donaldson ask. "What happened today Ms. Chamber?"

I didn't respond. I reached for the door handle, my eyes fixed on Reggie. I could still hear the sound of Officer Donaldson's voice but I had no idea of what he was saying. I got out of the car and started running towards Reggie. I was seeing red and had death in my eyes. I wanted him dead. I didn't want him to go to jail. Jail was too good for him after what he'd done to my baby. Just as I reached the sidewalk where he was Officer

Donaldson and another officer grabbed me.

"Calm down Ms. Chambers or we will have to arrest you!" The other officer barked at me. "From the looks of things, you may already be in a lot of trouble if Mr. Wade decides to press charges against you for assault."

"I don't give a fuck! Do whatever you have to do!" I yelled outraged as I struggled against them. "This sorry motherfucka touched my baby! I did what I had to do as a mother! I was protecting my child!" I continued struggling.

"Calm down Ms. Chambers!" Officer Donaldson said to me a lot more calm than the other officer had. His eyes were sympathetic and so was his tone. "I understand your anger. You have every right to be upset. I don't know anyone in their right mind who wouldn't want to do serious damage to him if they'd caught him doing to their child what he was doing to yours but you still have to try and gain control of yourself."

"I want him dead." I cried tears pouring from my eyes like water from a broken dam. I kept seeing Reggie stroking his erection and touching my baby. It played over and over in my head like a movie as I stared Officer Donaldson directly in the eyes. I trembled with anger. "He doesn't deserve to live after what he did. She's only a baby."

"Yes ma'am, I know that but you can't keep saying that either." He held onto me with a tight grip that I couldn't move from no matter how much I wanted to.

"It's true."

"Lala, I'm so sorry! I didn't mean to. You have to believe me. I never meant to hurt you or your kids." Reggie called to me as the officer and paramedic led him past me towards the ambulance. He wore what appeared to be a guilty expression as tears streamed down his cheeks. "I have an illness. Do you think I want to look at little kids in that way?"

Hearing his voice and seeing those fake ass tears

13

only infuriated me more. I started to struggle against the officers again. "Please let go of me!" I begged.

"Motherfucka, do you really want to cry? I can give your nasty no-good child molesting ass a reason to cry!"

"No." Officer Donaldson told me and then yelled to the officer that was assisting the paramedics with Reggie. "Hurry up and get that sack of shit out of here before I forget that I am an officer of the law and harm him myself! Scum like him disgust me!" He barked.

"Hmph, you aren't the only one." The other officer commented shaking his head. He looked at me. "We are going to allow you to take your daughter to the emergency room and have her checked out. Someone from Social Services will stop by to talk with you. I don't know who or when but they should be there shortly."

"Social services?" My heart dropped to my feet. I was confused. Were they trying to say that I was an unfit parent because I'd made one bad decision? "No...no one is taking my babies from me! This wasn't my fault! I had no idea that he was a pedophile! I would never have left them here with him if I'd thought that he would do something to hurt them. I had no idea, still that doesn't make me a bad mother!"

"Ma'am it is standard procedure when something like this occurs." Officer Donaldson told me. "After you are done at the hospital, you will need to come down to the police station."

"The police station?"

"Yes, I need to finish speaking with you about what happened. Can I trust you to come in on your own or will I be having to make a trip back here to pick you up?"

"No sir, I will come in on my own." I promised.

They turned me a loose and I went inside the house. Inside Nisey was sitting on the sofa holding Lola. She'd put some clothes on her. Laila was in her walker. I walked over and took Lola from Nisey's arms. I hugged her tightly rocking from side to side and just cried.

Lala

At the hospital the doctor did a complete examination of Lola and determined that there had been no penetration. I was thankful for that. He assured me that she was fine and let me know that it was okay for me to take her home. After dressing Lola, I walked out of the examination room headed to the waiting area where Nisey was with Laila to inform her that Lola was fine and that we could go.

When I walked into the hallway there was a petite black woman dressed in a brown pants suit standing next to the door holding a briefcase. Her thick coarse hair was pulled back into a bun. The silver hair around her hairline hinted her age. She wore a serious expression as she eyed me over the rim of her thick bifocals.

"Hello are you, LaQuela Chambers?" She pursed her thin lips and waited for my response.

"Yes ma'am, I am." I eyed the woman suspiciously

wondering why she'd been waiting outside the door and more importantly how she knew my name.

"Hmph, I see. My name is Marlene Reynolds." She extended her small hand to me and I slowly reached out and shook it. "I work for The Department of Social Services." She informed me. I immediately became nervous. "I am here to speak with you about the incident that took place earlier involving your daughter."

"O-Okay." I replied holding onto Lola a little tighter. I wasn't sure what I should expect but no one was taking either of my babies.

"We can go over there in that little area right there." She pointed to a small waiting area next to the nurse's station. "There's no one in there and we can have a little bit of privacy."

"Okay." I replied. That seem to be the only word that my brain could form at the moment because I was so distracted with wondering whether or not she was there to try and take my daughter.

She took the lead and I followed her into the small waiting area and took a seat in one of the comfortable leather chairs, placing Lola on my lap. She took a seat next to me leaving one seat empty between us. She placed her briefcase in the empty seat, opened it and took out a yellow pad and a pen.

"Okay, let's get started." She told me. "First could you please tell me your daughter's first and last name and her age?"

My mouth felt dry when I opened it and tried to speak. The first attempt nothing would come out. My nerves were getting the best of me. I swallowed hard and cleared my throat before attempting to speak again. "Her name is Lola Jefferson and she's eleven months old." My voice was low and shaky.

I sat and watched as she scribbled down the information that I'd just given her. Without looking up, she asked. "And you are the child's biological mother?"

"Yes ma'am."

"Father's name?"

"Tremaine Jefferson."

She looked up at me. "Reginald Wade is your boyfriend, correct?"

"Incorrect." I corrected her. "Reginald Wade was my boyfriend."

"At the time that this incident occurred earlier, Reginald Wade was your boyfriend. Correct?" She snapped.

"Yes but..."

She held up her hand. "Ms. Chambers all I need is a yes or a no and I believe that you have given me that." She scribbled something else on her notepad before looking back at me. "So tell me how long have you and Reginald been together?"

"Three months."

"How long have you known him?"

"Eleven months."

"How did the two of you meet?" I told her how

we'd met when I'd gone into labor. "I see...and does Mr. Wade live with you?"

"No ma'am, he lives in South Boston, VA. He comes to visit me every other weekend."

"And where is the father of the child?"

"He lives in Boykins, VA?"

"Does he know about the incident that occurred earlier?"

"Yes ma'am, I contacted him after I called the police."

"So tell me what happened earlier today." I told her the story from beginning to end. By the time that I was done, I was crying again. "Why didn't you take your daughters with you or why didn't you leave them with your best friend instead of both of you going to the store and leaving them with Mr. Wade? Has he ever babysat the girls before?" I wasn't sure of how I should take the disgusted look she was giving me or the snappy tone that she used to speak but I knew that things weren't looking too good for me.

"No, he's never babysat the girl's for me before. Today was the first time." I sniffled and used the back of my hand to wipe my runny nose. "I was going to take the girl's with Nisey and me to the grocery store but Reggie volunteered to watch them. He suggested that it would be better for me to leave them since Laila was asleep and I would be able to go and return a lot quicker without having to juggle the girls." I paused and took a deep breath, staring up at the ceiling I continued. "Ms. Reynolds…"

"It's *Mrs. Reynolds.*" She corrected me in the same snappy tone that she'd been using since we'd sat down.

I took another deep breath. I was already frustrated and nervous. I really didn't need her judgmental ass attitude on top of everything else. "Mrs. Reynolds…" I began again finally tearing my eyes away from the ceiling and looking her directly in her eyes. "I know that you don't know me and all you have to go off of is this one incident. I totally understand. I get that you are doing your job and I can respect that but while doing your job try to remember that as humans we sometimes make mistakes. We sometimes misjudge people's character because of what they show us. Reggie never showed me a bad side of him. He was always kind and respectful. I've never even witnessed the man raising his voice. That part of him he kept hidden very well. I realize that in this situation, I was very naïve. I was fooled by a wolf in sheep's clothing. That man has been preying on me since day one but I couldn't see it. I opened my door and allowed him into my home giving him access to my children. That is something that I will have to live with for the rest of my life. However, everything that has happened today has taught me a very valuable lesson and nothing like this will ever happen again. I love my daughter's more than anything. Anyone who knows me can verify that! I would've never left them with Reggie if I'd had any idea that he would do anything to harm either of them." I paused and wiped my tears and also repositioned Lola on my lap. "You can't imagine the relief I felt when that doctor told me that there had been no penetration. It was worse enough that he'd even touched her but I thank God that I'd left my pocketbook and went back when I did because this could've turned out so much worse. I look at this as a learning experience and you best believe I have learned my lesson. I hate so much that this happened…"

"Are you done with your little speech?" Mrs. Reynolds snapped rolling her eyes behind her glasses and letting out a frustrated breath.

"Excuse me?" I asked sitting up in my seat. This bitch's attitude was the worse and I wasn't sure how much longer I could deal with it before I slapped the shit out of her! The only thing that had been stopping me was knowing that if I touched her. I was no doubt going to jail and Social Services wouldn't hesitate to snatch my daughters. For those reasons, I kept telling myself that I had to remain calm.

"Listen, I am going to be totally honest with you." She started. "I have no sympathy or respect for women like you. You allow these men that you barely know to come into home around your children and then things like this occur. When you lay down and bring a child/children into this world your life is no longer about you, Ms. Chambers. That means every decision that you make affects your children but obviously you weren't thinking about your children when you allowed Mr. Wade into your home. All you were thinking about was how *kind, nice, and respectful* he seemed to be."

"Hold up, that's not fair. You have no right to sit up here and act as if I am some man-hungry female who puts a man before my children! You don't know me! I am a damn good mother to my children. I didn't bring this man into my home overnight. I'd known him for months." I checked her bougie ass! "How was I supposed to know that he was a pedophile?"

"While you had been knowing him for months did you ever visit him in South Boston? Ya know...get to know his family...learn a little bit about his background." She stared at me and waited for my answer.

"No but..."

"Exactly because had you taken the time to visit him and gotten to know a little bit about his background besides the fact that he was nice, kind and respectful Reggie. Maybe his sister could've told you that he'd spent four years in prison a while back for molesting her daughter!" She opened her briefcase and placed her pad and pen back inside. Then she stood with her briefcase in hand. "You'll be hearing from me soon. Sometime during the week." With that she strutted off down the hallway her heels making a loud clicking noise against the tile floor with every step that she took.

The news about Reggie molesting his own niece hit me like a ton of bricks! I sat there for several minutes after she'd left replaying everything over in my head.

"Lord what have I done? What kind of monster did I let into my home?" I asked aloud. "Please don't let them take my babies away. I realize that I made a huge mistake by allowing that man into my home but I don't know what I'd do if I lost my girls." I sat praying and holding on to Lola. I lifted her up and kissed her cheek. "Mama didn't mean for this to happen, Lola. I swear, I didn't. You know that don't you? I would never do anything to hurt you or your sister." She stared at me as if she was trying to understand what I was saying. "I promise you that nothing like this will ever happen again. I will never leave you or Laila alone with another man unless it's your daddy."

At the mention of Tre, I realized that he should be arriving soon if he hadn't already. I gathered Lola in my arms and made my way out of the waiting area. We went down the hall to the main waiting area where Nisey was waiting with Laila. I looked around but there was no sign of Tre.

"Tre hasn't made it yet." Nisey informed me obviously knowing who I was looking for.

"Oh okay...I'm ready." I told her. "I still have to go by the police station."

She stood placing Laila on her hip. "Is everything okay with Lola-Bug?" She asked reaching out and playing with Lola's hand.

"Yeah, she's fine. The doctor said that there was no sign of penetration. That's a relief. I can only imagine what that sick..." My voice cracked and I couldn't continue.

Nisey wrapped her free arm around me. "Shhh...don't cry Lala. Everything is going to be alright." She did her best to comfort me. "I hope they put his sick ass beneath the prison! I also hope that a group of guys fuck him in his ass until his sorry no good ass croaks over!"

"Nisey, I am so scared." I wiped my eyes with trembling fingers and looked up at her. "I spoke with a social worker while I was back there. She had a real nasty ass attitude and from the way she was talking, I think she's going to try and take my babies. She acted like I meant for this to happen. She said that I should've taken more time to get to know Reggie before letting him into my home."

"Damn you had known him for a minute before y'all hooked up!" Nisey snapped smacking her lips and rolling her eyes. "How long did she want you to wait?"

I shrugged my shoulders. "I wish that I had checked him out a little bit more now. She said that Reggie had been in prison before for molesting his niece."

"What?" Nisey all but yelled. "What the hell? Ol' nasty motherfucka! Uh-uhh!"

I shook my head and let out a sigh. "Nisey what have I done?"

"You didn't do anything! You can't blame yourself for the fact that he is trifling as hell going around touching babies. You and I both know that you are a good mother to your babies and I don't give a damn what that social workers says. I don't know too many people who go out and dig up a person's entire history before they start dating them."

"Nah but..."

"There is no but. This isn't your fault." She told me in a stern voice looking me in my eyes and then grabbing a hold of my hand. "Now come on so that we can swing by the police station and then get these babies home. It's been a long crazy day."

We left the hospital and went to the police station. At the police station, I gave them a full statement about what had happened earlier.

"Okay Ms. Chambers, we appreciate your cooperation and I want you to know that I am truly sorry for what happened to your daughter. You have to be very careful about the people that you let come around your children." Detective Ross, a short chubby man, told me.

"The good news is that Mr. Wade refuses to press charges against you…"

"Press charges against me?" I jumped to my feet. "What the hell do you mean? He touched my baby! I had every right to do what I did to him! I should've done more!"

"Calm down Ms. Chambers. Take your seat." He said calmly. I did as I was told but I was still fuming. "Now like I was saying. Mr. Wade refuses to press charges against you for assault, which he has every right to do even though he was in the wrong. He has admitted to touching your daughter and has been charged with the following and is being held with no bond as of right now but that could change once he goes in front of the judge on Monday." He read off all of Reggie's charges to me.

When he was done, I asked. "Is that all?" I was more than ready to get out of there and go home.

"Yes ma'am. I will call you if I need any further information from you."

I didn't reply. I got up and pushed my chair beneath the table that I had been sitting at and exited the room. I couldn't believe that the law was so fucked up that a child molester had the option to press charges against me for defending my child!

Tre

When I arrived at Tyson's crib, I threw the car in park and jumped out. I was so pissed that I couldn't even remember the drive there! I ran up the steps, skipping a few on the way. When I reached the front door I didn't bother ringing the doorbell. I banged on the door like a madman!

"Yo Tyson! Tyson its Tre open up yo!" I yelled as I continued to bang. I'd told him to be ready when I got there but he obviously hadn't done like I'd asked because if he had his ass would've been standing by the road waiting!

The door opened and Ms. Jackie stood there wearing a scared/confused look on her face and her hair sticking straight up on top of her head. "Tre...what in the world is wrong with you banging and carrying on like that out here? I have neighbors, son."

"Where is Tyson?" I asked ignoring the bullshit that had just come from her mouth. I didn't give a flying fuck about her neighbors. They could all kiss my black ass and so could she.

"He's..."

Before she could respond, Tyson appeared in the doorway behind her. "Here I go bruh, you ready to ride?" The expression on his face resembled the one that I wore on mine. I'd briefed him on what had happened over the phone.

"Where are you going Tyson?" Ms. Jackie asked looking from him to me.

He brushed past her and walked out onto the porch fixing his shirt. "I'm going to ride with Tre somewhere. I'll be back."

I turned and started to walk down the steps. From behind me, I heard Ms. Jackie say. "Uh-uhh, I don't know what kind of trouble he is mixed up in now but you aren't going anywhere behind him and end up in a world of trouble! Whatever he's gotten himself into let him handle it himself!"

I turned around and charged back up the steps. I was so sick of this bitch's mouth! She'd picked the wrong day to come out of her face wrong. With the mood that I was in, I was liable to flip out and beat the life out of her ass and be ready to deal with Tyson next because frankly I didn't give a fuck about anything or anybody. "Look if you don't know what you are talking about then..."

"Chill Tre, man. I got this." Tyson met me before I had a chance to reach Ms. Jackie.

"Uh-uhhh...I know you don't call yourself running up on me!" Ms. Jackie raised her voice and started towards me. "Boy, I have been knowing your little ass since before you knew yourself! I wish you would get up in my face! I will slap the piss from you and tell your mammy I did it! That's what's wrong with y'all little young punks. You don't have any damn respect but trust and believe me you are going to learn some today if you run up on me wrong. Let him go Tyson!"

"Ma, chill out! You're wrong. You are popping off when you don't even know what you are talking about. He ain't even did shit. Something happened to his daughter and I am about to ride with him to check on her." He explained to Ms. Jackie who was fuming mad. I watched as she eyed me with an evil mug on her face.

She rolled her eyes at me. "He still doesn't have any right to be disrespectful." She snapped.

"You started with me! Every damn time that I come here, you come out of your mouth wrong at me and I take it. In case you didn't know respect goes two ways." I let her know. "You had no idea why I'd come to get Tyson but you just assumed that I was in some kind of trouble. Even if I was I don't need him to fight my battles. I am a grown ass man and I can handle myself. Just like Tyson is a grown ass man. I didn't ask him to go with me. He volunteered to go, that was his decision." She didn't say anything she just stood there looking at me. She was probably feeling stupid for assuming some shit and not knowing what the hell she was talking about. Either way, I didn't have time for this shit. I needed to get to Danville. I looked at Tyson. "What are you going to do? Are you riding with me or what?"

"Yeah man." He turned his attention to Ms. Jackie. "Ma, I'll be back later on." He said leaning in and giving her a peck on her cheek.

I walked to the car and got inside. Tyson walked off the porch and hopped in on the other side. As we were backing out of the driveway, Ms. Jackie yelled. "Don't bring your black ass back in my yard no more Tre!"

I didn't bother replying, instead I rolled up the window and turned up the radio. Out of the corner of my eye, I saw Tyson remove the gun from his waist and slip it into my glove box. We'd gotten a few miles up the road when my phone started to ring. I picked it up and looked at the screen. It was Mina, for a split second I started not to answer but I pressed send anyways.

"Yeah…" I answered hoping that she didn't say anything out of her mouth that would further piss me off.

"You were mad as hell when you left. I was calling to see if you were okay." She explained.

I'd been at her place when Lala had called. The two of us were talking about our relationship or lack thereof. I really hadn't been feeling her as much since the whole incident at Ms. Lizzie's. I could tell by how insecurely that she'd reacted, she had a lot of shit going on. I didn't have time to try and pacify her feelings and emotions. I wasn't about to try and piece back together what the nigga before me had torn apart. I was with her and I showed that. Yet every time Lala or Kisha called my phone she seemed to get in her feelings. I'd explained to her time and time again that I had kids with both of them and that they were going to be a part of my life forever. She was going to have to accept that or move on.

"Nah, I'm not okay but I will be as soon as I make it

to Danville."

"What's that supposed to mean?" She asked. "What in the world did Lala call and tell you?"

"Look, I don't really feel up to doing a whole lot of talking right now. I'm not trying to be mean but I am pissed right now and I don't want to take it out on you so let me hit you back later."

"Okay, Tre be careful and don't go and get yourself in any trouble." I didn't reply, I just disconnected the call. I noticed that I had an unread text message. I opened it and saw that it was from Lala. It read: *The doctor said that Lola is fine. There was no signs of penetration so that means that he only touched her. Thank God for that. I will call you when I leave the police station.* I tossed my phone in the cup holder and pressed down harder on the accelerator.

Tyson reached over and turned down the radio. "Are you alright man?" He asked looking over at me. Before I could reply, he spoke again. "Don't sweat that shit that moms was saying. You know how that goes. She be buggin' sometimes but it comes from a good place though." He pulled out a blunt from his pocket and pushed in the lighter.

"It is what it is to be real with you." I answered looking straight ahead but to be honest I wasn't even really paying attention to the road. At this point, it was by the grace of God that we hadn't had an accident or been pulled over by the police because I was going way over the speed limit and passing everything on the road. "Right now that shit that your mama said is the furthest thing from my mind. All I am concerned about is getting to Danville and making sure that my baby is okay before I go looking for Reggie's bitch ass!"

Tyson touched the lighter to the end of the blunt and inhaled before putting the lighter back. "I feel you man." He said releasing smoke through his nose and mouth. He went into a coughing fit for a few seconds and then continued. "On some real shit though, how did this happen? I mean, was he staying there and snuck into the baby's room or did she leave them there with him while she went to work? What the fuck happened?" He reached over and handed me the blunt. I took it from his hand and took a long pull inhaling the smoke into my lungs. I needed something to calm my nerves and relax me some.

"Man, she said that she left them with him so that she could run to the grocery store but she'd left her purse and when she came back to get it. She caught him touching Lola." Visions of Reggie touching Lola flooded my mind and I nearly lost control of the wheel. I swerved into the next lane almost side swiping a truck but was able to get back in my lane in time to avoid it.

"Pull over and let me drive!" Tyson ordered. I could tell by the look on his face that I'd scared the shit out of him. "You ain't in no shape to be driving."

A few miles up the road, I pulled over and allowed him to drive. I slid into the passenger seat, turned the radio back up and reclined my seat. For the rest of the drive, I was quiet, in my own world consumed by my thoughts. From the way that I was lying back in my seat, I could see the sky. It was cloudy, the sky had turned a dark grey and it looked as if we were about to get some rain. The weather was like a reflection of my life at the moment, dark and cloudy and for some reason the rain hadn't let up. It'd constantly been one thing after another. Whenever I felt like things were getting better something else would happen and it always involved either Lala or Kisha. I'd thought that not being with either of them would change that but obviously not because no matter what happened in their lives I was still involved.

My thoughts went to Lala's phone call. I thought back to how she'd said Reggie ended up alone with Lola. I couldn't understand why she would leave our daughter in some other nigga's care! Just because she was fuckin' him didn't make that nigga trustworthy enough to be babysitting my kids. I shook my head and ran my hands over my face before sitting my seat up. I prayed to God that I calmed down some before I made it to Danville because if not there was no telling what I might do to Lala or Reggie.

As soon as I saw the sign that read WELCOME TO DANVILLE, I turned down the radio, took out my cell and found Lala's name in my contacts. I pressed her name on my touch screen, placed the phone to my ear and waited for her to answer. She answered after several rings, sounding tired and out of breath.

"Hey...sorry it took so long to answer. We are just getting back home." She explained.

"I'm in Danville, on my way to your crib now." I hung up because I really didn't feel like hearing her voice. I reached in the console that was between the seats and took out my cigarettes. I lit one up and focused my attention on the road so I could give Tyson the directions to Lala's house.

"Tre, I've been doing some thinking on the drive

man." Tyson started. "More than likely they done locked that nigga up by now. So what do you plan to do?"

I looked over at him. That thought had crossed my mind as well. When I'd initially called him and asked him for his gun, I hadn't thought about how long it was going to take us to actually make it to Danville. I'd been reacting out of anger. "I don't know but he'd better hope like hell that they have him locked up because if they let him out his ass is mine." I answered truthfully. "To be perfectly honest with you. The way that I am feeling Lala's ass could get it at this point."

I saw his head snap around in my direction like he couldn't believe the words that had just come from my mouth. "W-what? What do you mean, Lala could get it?" He asked glancing at the road and then back at me. A look of confusion covered his face as he tried to concentrate on the road and look at me at the same time. "Man, I understand that you are upset but you are buggin' now. I ain't bring no gun for you to use on your babymama. For that fuck boy...yeah...but her...hell nah!"

"Yo, get over in the left lane and make this left up here at the light." I instructed.

He did as he was told but he wasn't letting go of my last statement easily. "Tre, I know that she made a fucked up decision by leaving your kids with that nigga but it ain't her fault. It's his fault, he knew better! I'm not saying that you shouldn't be upset with her but not to the point where you are talking reckless."

"Make another left right up here after you pass this gas station." I continued to ignore what he was saying about Lala. In my opinion Lala wasn't shit and her life didn't mean shit to me!

"Tre, do you hear what I am saying?" He raised his voice but I didn't reply I just looked straight ahead. He stopped on brakes in the middle of the street causing the tires to screech and both of us to jerk forward. Luckily, I was wearing my seat belt.

"What the fuck is wrong with you, yo?" I roared

reaching over and shoving him in the chest! Car horns blared from behind us.

He shoved me back hard in the chest! "I asked you a motherfuckin' question? Did you hear anything that I was saying to you? I am not about to take you over here to this girl's house and be partially responsible for you fucking her up!" He barked pointing a finger in my face.

"Either drive this motherfucka or you can get the fuck out and I will drive it my gotdamn self! Fuck that bitch!" I banged my fist on the dashboard! "She is responsible for that nigga touching my baby and if you ask me, she is just as much to blame as him!"

The cars behind us were blowing their horns relentlessly. He started to drive again slowly. "Tre, you need to calm down and think rationally before you do something that you may regret. I understand that you are upset and I would be too." I could hear the sympathy in his voice. I knew without a doubt that he was saying all of the things that he was out of love for me. He was in the car right now with me because he loved me. His getting in the car and bringing the gun that I'd asked for said everything. He'd been willing to risk his own freedom for my daughter. I let out a frustrated breath and looked out the window. "I'm sure that she regrets her decision to leave those babies with him more than you or I could ever imagine. You told me out of your own mouth that she is a good mother and that she takes good care of those girls. Didn't you?"

"Yeah…" I replied still looking out the window. "Don't forget to make this right up here."

"I got this. You just listen to what I am telling you before you end up in jail." He told me. "Your babies have been through enough for one day."

I let the things that he was saying sink in. He was making a lot of sense and I knew that I should take heed to what he was saying. He was right I didn't want to end up in jail and I didn't want to show up and act a fool in front of my kids. I took a deep breath and exhaled slowly.

Then I did the same thing again. "I'm good." I told him

just as we were coming up to Lala's house. "It's that

house right there." I pointed.

Tre

I walked up on the porch with Tyson right behind me. I rang the bell twice and waited. There were two cars parked in Lala's driveway, one I knew belonged to her friend Nisey but I wasn't sure of who the other one belonged to. My mind was telling me that it more than likely belonged to Reggie.

"Shit, I left my cigarettes in the car." I told Tyson patting my pockets as if I were really looking for my cigarettes. I walked off the porch and jogged back to the car. I opened the glove box, took out the gun and slipped it in the waist of my pants. Then I grabbed my cigarettes and headed back towards the porch.

Just as I was walking up the steps, I heard the sound of the door being unlocked. The door opened slowly and Lala stood on the other side.

"Hey, come on in." She told us. Her eyes were red and puffy from all of the crying that she'd done. Seeing her puffy eyes only made me heated all over again. It was her poor ass judgment that had led to all of this.

I walked past her and into the house. I went into the living room and saw Nisey sitting on the sofa. "Hey." I spoke, my eyes roaming over the room. I saw blood stains on the carpet and the knick knacks that normally sat on the coffee table were strolled about the floor.

"Hey, Tre." She replied wearing a tired expression. She was leaning back with her shoes off and her feet up on the sofa. She took her feet down as we were walking into the room.

"What's up?" Tyson spoke.

"Hey." She greeted him as well.

"Where are the girls?" I turned around and looked at Lala after I didn't see either of them.

"They're in their room asleep." She answered taking a seat on the sofa down from Nisey. Tyson had taken a seat in the chair across from the sofa.

"Where did that blood come from on the floor?" I knew that she'd texted me that Lola was fine but I wanted to be sure.

"Reggie's." She answered rubbing her temples.

I walked out of the room and went down the hallway to the girl's room. I walked over to Laila's crib. She was sleeping so peacefully, like a little angel. It was amazing to me how she and Lola seemed to be the perfect combination of Lala and me. With the boys they looked exactly like me but it wasn't like that with the girls. I leaned over and kissed her on her cheek and then fixed her little blanket. Next I walked over to Lola. She always slept with one of her hands over her face. I'd always found it to be so cute. I stood there for a minute and just watched her, thinking to myself how she'd been through quite a bit since she'd come into the world. First there was the condition with her heart and now this bullshit. I couldn't help but wonder what kind of sick motherfucka would want to harm an innocent child who has no way of defending themselves. I shook my head. I felt warm tears roll down my cheeks and reached up to wipe them away. I found a little comfort in knowing that Lala had returned before Reggie had gotten the opportunity to actually molest her but just the thought of him having the audacity to touch her caused my anger to boil over.

I left out of the girl's bedroom and headed back into the living room, tears steadily streaming from my eyes. I couldn't ever remember being so upset about anything in my life and I couldn't remember the last time that anything had brought tears from my eyes. I began to fear what I might end up doing at this point. I wasn't sure of how much longer I could control my anger before I flipped out.

"Where is Reggie at now?" I asked walking back into the living room. I used my hand to wipe my face but it didn't seem to help. My mind was fucking with me hard because I couldn't get those crazy images of Reggie touching Lola to go away. I shook my head and ran my hand over my face again.

"You good?" Tyson asked looking at me strangely. "Maybe we should step outside and get some air."

"I'm good man." I assured him. I looked over at Lala. "Where is he?"

"He's in jail. The detective said that he's being held without bond but that could change Monday when he goes before the judge." She let out a sigh. "I hope and pray that they don't give him a bond. His ass needs to rot in there."

"Nah they need to let that nigga out!" I barked spittle flying from my mouth. "Jail is too good for him! They need to let me handle him. A nigga like him doesn't deserve to live, going around touching babies and shit!"

"Hmph, same damn thing I said." Nisey added sucking her teeth. "Lala said that the social worker told her this isn't the first time that he's touched a kid. The last time it was his niece!"

Hearing that took me over the edge! "Say what? This motherfucka has done this shit before?" I charged towards Lala. She jumped back, looking scared to death. She held her hands up like she was afraid that I was going to hit her and I can't lie it did cross my mind. "All this time you had a fuckin child molester laying up in here with my kids? What in the fuck is wrong with you?"

"I didn't know!" She yelled bursting into tears and covering her face with her hands. "How was I supposed to know?"

"You're right you couldn't have known but you did know that nigga wasn't their daddy! Why in the fuck did you leave my kids with him in the first gotdamn place?" I didn't give her a chance to answer. "You should've taken them with you!"

She removed her hands from her face. Her face was wet with tears and snot. "Don't you think that I realize that now?" She screamed. "Do you know how many times today that I've wished that I could take back my decision to leave them here with him but I can't Tre! I can't!" She stopped talking and sobbed loudly.

"Tre, man...y'all chill out. Yelling and screaming at each other isn't going to solve anything." Tyson attempted to be the voice of reason, which was also starting to get on my nerves. At this point I didn't want to hear words of reason! Fuck that! People always seem to have the answers when it's not their situation. If he were in my shoes he would probably be reacting in the same way or worse. "Let's just be thankful that Lil Mama is alright."

"Tre, I really didn't mean for this to happen." Lala sniffled. She'd pulled herself together some. "I know that I am partially to blame because I should've never left them here with Reggie alone but you have to know that I would never do anything to hurt my babies. I love those two girls more than anything in this world..." Her voice cracked and she seemed to be struggling to get her words out. "I'd die for those two girls."

"Shhh...don't cry, Lala. We all know that you love those babies." Nisey said getting up and moving closer to Lala. She reached over and rubbed her back. She shot me a nasty look. "Nobody is perfect, we all make mistakes and use poor judgment at times but sometimes people tend to forget all of their mistakes and moments of poor judgment when they are busy pointing the finger at us playing the blame game. All of a sudden their imperfections become nonexistent but oh as soon as they fuck up again they are always the main ones begging for others to have understanding, be forgiving and realize that they aren't perfect. Funny how they can't do the same thing."

I knew that bitch was hinting at how things had gone down in the beginning between Lala and I when the twins were first born. Yeah, I'd done some pretty foul shit but it couldn't be compared to Lala leaving my daughters with her child molesting ass boyfriend! I didn't respond to the slick shit that Nisey had just said because I knew that if she said something else slick in response, I was going to take her head right off of her body. To me that shit she was poppin' didn't even deserve a response. I paced back and forth trying to calm myself down.

"This is why, I wanted us to try and work things out between us so that we could be a family." Lala was still sniffling. "That way no other man would be around our kids and we wouldn't have to worry about anything like this ever happening but you didn't want that."

Her last statement caused me to lose what little bit of self-control that I had left. "Bitch what do you mean, *but you didn't want that!* Don't try and make this shit about you and me!" I roared pointing my finger in her face. "This shit is about you and your fucked up decision to leave our daughters with a nigga who you apparently barely even knew! Bottom line is you should've taken them with you!"

"I am not making this about us! I was just saying!"

"Saying what exactly? That this shit is somehow my fault?"

"I'm saying that this could've been avoided if you and I had given raising our daughters together a try. You obviously blame me for this. That's basically what you've been saying since you got here but honestly I never wanted to bring another man into my home with my daughters. I wanted it to be you and me but when you told me that wasn't going to happen. I moved on. I had no idea that I was moving on to someone like that but realistically no one goes and do a full background check on the people they date. I judged him according to the man that he showed me when he was with me. From what I saw he was never violent in anyway." She explained. "It's not like he was drooling over little girls right before my eyes or like there were any clues. Unfortunately there are people like Reggie everywhere. We communicate with them every day and have no idea. This incident taught me some very valuable lessons. I know that I have to be more careful and trust no one around my children. Trust me, you don't ever have to worry about this happening again."

"You're damn sure right about that because when I leave Laila and Lola will be leaving with me." I informed her. "I never know when you will need to run out to the grocery store again and being that I didn't chose to be here with you and them, there's no telling who you will leave them with this time." I turned and started towards the girl's room so that I could start packing their things because there was no way I was leaving them.

"Nooo..." I heard Lala cry out from behind me and then she was coming after me. "Tre, you are not taking my babies anywhere." She grabbed a hold of my shirt and I snatched away from her and continued walking down the hallway. "Tre, no...stop! Why are you doing this?" She grabbed my shirt again and I snatched away again. Just as I was about to open the door to the girl's room. I felt a blow to the back of the head and then there was another!

I spun around and slapped her so hard that she fell back into the wall. I grabbed her by her hair and started banging her head against the wall. "You trifling bitch! Don't you ever put your motherfuckin' hands on me again!" I yelled before turning her hair a loose and slapping the shit out of her two more times. Without thinking I reached into the waist of my pants, pulled out the gun and aimed it at her. "Bitch, I should splatter your motherfuckin' brains all over this hallway! You are a sorry excuse for a fuckin' human being. I have absolutely no respect at all left for you."

She coward against the wall in the corner with her hands covering her head, trembling and crying. "Tre please...please don't..." She begged.

"Man, gotdamn it! What are you doing?" Tyson yelled. "Nigga what the fuck? Give me the motherfuckin' gun Tre!" He demanded but I didn't budge. All I kept thinking was how much I hated Lala at that moment and how Reggie was locked up and I had no way of getting to him and making him pay for what he had done. She was the next best thing. "Tre give me the gotdamn gun! What are you going to do? Stand here and shoot your kid's mother for a fuckin' mistake? What is that going to prove except that you ain't no better than the motherfucka' that's locked up for touching your daughter? That is exactly what those two little girls are going to think of you if you take their mother from them."

"Fuck you!" I spat turning the gun on him. "You are talking a lot of shit for someone who's empty handed."

"I don't give a fuck about that shit. I'd rather you shoot me than that girl. She has two kids to raise but obviously you don't give a fuck about that." He didn't back down. He spoke staring me straight in my eyes wearing a fearless expression. "You're wrong Tre."

I looked over at Lala who was still sitting in the corner crying and staring at me scared to death. Then I looked back at Tyson. "You don't understand man." I shook my head and wiped tears from my eyes.

"I do understand but this right here ain't the way to handle this shit."

I lowered the gun and Tyson took it from my hands. He put the safety back on and placed it in the waist of his jeans. "Come on let's go outside for a few minutes."

I was about to reply when I caught a blow directly across my face! Nisey had snuck my ass! "You bitch ass motherfucka! How you gone pull a gun on your children's mother!" She swung again and connected with my nose. Tyson quickly got between us. "I been told Lala that you weren't shit!" She screamed over Tyson's shoulder jumping up trying to get another lick in. "Motherfucka, you want to run up in here placing blame! Where in the fuck were you in the beginning when she was doing everything by her damn self? You weren't concerned then with who she had around your babies! If my memory serves me correctly Reggie's child molesting ass was sniffing around back then too but I guess it didn't matter then because ol girl that you was living with didn't know about Lala and *your* babies! Now all of a sudden you are a changed man and got your shit together, you done forgot all of the foul shit you did to *your* babies!"

"Bitch this ain't got shit to do with you!" I barked struggling against Tyson to get to Nisey!

"Let his ass go!" She challenged. "There ain't a bitch walking and bleeds every month that I'm afraid of! And that's exactly what he is...a bitch!"

"Yo, chill the fuck out Shorty!" Tyson told her trying to hold onto me and push me down the hallway at the same time. "Tre, chill!"

"Nah, he didn't have to pull a gun on her!" She replied. "It's all good though, I got something for your ass! I'm going to see if you pull that same gun on the police!"

"No Nisey...please don't call the police!" Lala begged. "Please...put the phone away. I don't want any more police coming to my house today. All I need is for us fighting or that someone had a gun in the house with the kids to get back to that social worker and she will sure as hell be in here trying to snatch my kids. She's already trying to play me like I'm an unfit mother."

"Are you crazy? That motherfucka just beat your ass and pulled a gun on you!" Nisey told her. "All of that because you made a mistake? He has no right to blame you for this shit and neither does that bitch!"

"I have every right to blame her and you too!" I let her know. "You mean to tell me neither one of y'all grown asses second guessed leaving my kids with him!" Nisey didn't respond. I guess her ignorant ass realized that I had a point.

"Tre, just leave. All I want for you to do is leave!" Lala cried. I could see that her lip was busted and swollen. "I won't call the police...I promise. Please just leave."

"I will leave but not without my kids."

"You are not taking my babies!" She tried to sound stern but she was still too shaken up and probably too afraid of what I might do to her ass if she didn't back the fuck up.

"Watch me!" I jerked away from Tyson and walked past Lala and Nisey. My eyes were fixed on Nisey hoping that she would act like she was about to swing but she didn't she just ice grilled me. I think the part of her brain that worked properly was telling her not to fuck with me because she might lose her life over some shit that wasn't even her business. I went into the girl's room and turned on the light. I picked Lola up out of her bed and then walked over and scooped Laila up. I didn't give a damn about their clothes. I'd buy them some more. I turned to walk out of the room but Lala stood blocking the doorway. She looked up at me with hurt filled eyes, tears steadily streaming down her face.

"Why are you doing this?" She asked her voice was hoarse. "I can't allow you to take my babies." She shook her head. "I can't…"

"You don't have a choice, these are my kids too." I replied coldly. All of the crying that she was doing didn't faze me one bit. Fuck her tears. "It's getting late and we have a long ride head of us."

"Tre, please…"

"Please my ass…now move." I snapped. "Right now, I don't trust your judgment so they are going to stay with me for a while. You can see them anytime that you want but as far as them staying here…nah…that's not happening. Ain't no telling what other type of niggas you will have around them. I can't afford for no shit like this to happen again. Maybe you should consider moving back to Boykins because that is the only way I am going to allow you to have them back."

"Will you please stop acting like I meant for this to happen?"

"It could've been avoided." I replied. "Now move or I will move you. I am not about to stand here and go back and forth with you."

Wearing a look of exhaustion and defeat she moved back out of the way. "Tre, you are dead wrong for this."

"I'll be that." I replied over my shoulder. "Think about what I said, if you want them back. You will have to move back to Boykins because they will not be coming back here." She followed me down the hallway begging and pleading but it only fell on deaf ears. "Where are their car seats?"

"Tre...don't"

"Bitch tell me where their car seats are!" I said through clenched teeth. This shit ain't up for discussion!"

"Lala please give him the car seats and their diaper bags." Tyson told her. "I know you don't want him to take them but as you can see there is no reasoning with him tonight. Give him a little time to cool off and then y'all can talk but that isn't going to happen tonight."

She looked defeated. "I didn't mean for this to

happen. I swear...I didn't."

"I believe you." He told her.

"That's nice but where in the fuck is the car seats?" I barked becoming agitated with Tyson playing like he was Dr. Phil or some shit!

"They are in my car, it's unlocked." Lala told me and then hung her head and walked out of the room. I heard her bedroom door closed. Nisey looked at me and rolled her eyes before walking out. She went down the hall to check on her, I assume because I heard a door close a few seconds later. I gathered all of the things that I needed for the girls and then we left. The drive back was quiet, I assumed that Tyson was feeling some kind of way about how I'd handled things but I truly didn't give a damn.

Mina

I stood working on my client's hair and thinking about the brief conversation that Tre and I had just had. He'd called me a few minutes ago asking if I could do something to the twin's hair for him. At first I'd been confused because I knew that Quan and Shaun didn't have any hair and to my knowledge the girls were in Danville with their mama. Apparently something really serious had gone down in Danville the day before because Tre now had the girl's with him. I'd asked him what was going on but he'd just said he didn't want to talk about it so I hadn't pressed the issue any further. Instead, I'd agreed to stop by his house and do the girl's hair for him when I got off work.

"Why are you so quiet over there Mina?" Nelle asked looking up from her client's hair. "Ever since you got off the phone you have been quiet and looking into space. You lookin' like somebody just told you some real ish." She laughed.

"Nah, I am just trying to figure out what is going on with Tre and his babymama, girl." I rolled my eyes thinking to myself how there was always something going on with either Lala or Kisha. I tried my best not to say anything and stay in my lane but those two bitches irked my nerves to the point of no return always blowing up Tre's phone day and night. He swore up and down that they were always calling about something pertaining to the kids but I wasn't believing that shit. Granted, Mello was locked up but even if he wasn't I couldn't see why I would need to call him constantly about our daughter. I mean, Lala and Kisha were both ridiculous with it. Lala called if the girls took a piss or shit because she claimed that she didn't want Tre to miss out on anything. And Kisha always seem to need something for the boys. I am all for a man taking care of his kids and I have to say that Tre was one of the best dad's that I've ever seen but in my opinion Kisha needed to get up off of her lazy ass and get a fucking job and stop depending on Tre for everything. Shit they were her kids too.

"What do you mean, you are trying to figure out what is going on with Tre and his babymama?" Nelle continued to pry. "And which babymama are you talking about anyways?"

"Lala. She called Tre yesterday while the two of us were at my crib chillin' and talking. I have no idea what the call was about but I did make out that she was upset and crying. Then again she and Kisha always are crying with their super dramatic asses." I replied rolling my eyes. "Whatever she said was going on must've been serious because he jumped up like there was a fire somewhere and all but ran out of the house but then again when it comes to either one of them, that's how he always react."

"So he still hasn't bothered to tell you what happened?"

"Nah but he called me just now and asked if I could stop by after I get off from work and do something to the girl's hair for him." I reached over and picked up a few Bobbie pins so that I could pin up my client's hair. "Girrrl...whatever happened in Danville must've been really bad for him to bring the girl's back. And his exact words were, '*I need you to do something to their hair that will last for a while because I am going to have them for a minute and I don't know shit about no hair and neither does my mama.*' That tells me that Lala didn't come back with them."

"Hmmmm...child some shit done went down and I am going to need for you to get all of the details so that you can fill me in tomorrow."

I burst out laughing. "Girl, you are a hot mess but

you know that I am. I can't wait to get off, go over to his house and find out the scoop."

"Y'all both need Jesus." Mia gave her two cents as she gathered her things. She picked up her pocketbook and slung it over her shoulder. "There could be something seriously wrong and y'all two chickens can't wait to hear what it is so y'all can gossip about it." She sucked her teeth. "That's why I try my best to keep my business to myself because y'all will spread anybody's business."

"Child, what crawled up your ass and has you all in a funk?" Nelle asked looking at Mia confused. Mia didn't reply so she looked over at me and mouthed. "What's her problem?"

I just shrugged my shoulders and continued to work on my client's hair. Mia really hadn't had much for me to do since the whole incident with Corey. I was so afraid that she might say something to Nelle that I didn't bother to press the issue about the change in her attitude towards me. I just let things be because I didn't want to piss her off and there be a big mess. I knew that she wouldn't hesitate to tell Nelle how she'd caught me eyeing Corey.

After gathering all of her belongings, Mia said good bye to everyone and headed for the door but Nelle stopped her just before she made it out the door.

"Are you good cuzzo?" Nelle asked her. "Why are you leaving?"

"I'm good." Mia assured with her hand on the door knob. "I have a doctor's appointment in forty-five minutes, that's why I'm leaving."

"Oh alright. Well call me later and let me know how everything went." Nelle smiled. "Are you sure everything is good? You look annoyed. I know you aren't that upset over a lil gossip."

Mia waved Nelle off and gave her what looked to be a forced smile. "Nah, I'm not upset at all. It doesn't have anything to do with me."

"Oh alright."

"I'll call you later." With that she left.

"Is it just me or has Mia been acting a little different lately?" Nelle asked once Mia was gone. "I mean, she always seem to have an attitude about something."

"To be honest, I really haven't paid her that much attention." I lied knowing that Mia's attitude had definitely changed and also knowing the reason for it. "Girl, there has been so much going on with Tre and I that I haven't paid attention to much other than the mess that we have going on."

"Hmph, well I don't see how in the world you could miss how she has been acting. It's like she's mad with the world about something. She definitely hasn't been herself lately." Nelle continued on about Mia. The look on her face told that she was really concerned about what was going on with her. "Maybe I should try talking to her? I don't like to see my fam like that."

When she mentioned talking to her my heart

skipped a beat. All I could think about was Mia telling her about the little Corey situation. "Nah maybe you should just give her a little time and see if she will come to you about whatever it is that is bothering her." She gave me a strange look so I explained. "I'm just saying, she just said that she doesn't like telling us her business because we love to gossip. If you go to her and ask her what is going on. She may feel like you are only trying to be nosey so that you can spread her business."

Nelle smacked her lips. "Mia knows that I would never do anything foul like that. Yeah, I heard what she said but at the end of the day, I know that she knows that I would never spread her business around. I don't cross my fam." She shook her head, her micros swaying back and forth. "Nah, that ain't how I get down."

"You know that, I know that." I told her. "And Mia should know that but obviously she believes that you would. She did say 'y'all spread everybody's business.' She didn't just say me."

"I don't care what she said. She knows that I wouldn't do that. Hell, I've never done it before. She just said that mess because of whatever she has going on."

"Maybe…but don't say that I didn't warn you." I was tired of talking about Mia so I changed the subject. "So how are things with you and my favorite cousin-in-law?" I pried. Even after the incident with Mia catching me eyeing Corey, I still had it bad for him. He was one of those people that you wonder what it would be like to be with them at least once. I wanted so badly to be with Corey just one time. I'd been admiring him from afar for years now and to be very honest I was tired of just looking, lusting and wondering. I wanted to find out what it was about him that had Nelle so in love that whenever he walked into a room her entire face lit up and just the mention of his name caused her lips to spread into a smile that nearly touched both ears. And I definitely couldn't forget how he'd driven the white chic that he'd met in DC so crazy that she'd tried to kill Nelle and his mama. It didn't make things any better having to see his fine ass nearly every day. That only made it worse.

"Things with Corey and I aren't too good right now but I am not letting it get to me. We will be alright." She sighed moving one of her braids back out of her face. "My baby is seriously pissed at me. We had a pretty heated argument this morning." She gave a little pouty face, poking out her lips.

That got my attention. Since everything that had gone down with Amy, the two of them rarely argued. That situation actually appeared to have worked in their favor because they had become inseparable and almost like some hood love fairy-tale.

"Mad at you, for what?" I pried with raised brows, waiting for her response. I'd even stopped working on my client's hair. I didn't want to miss a word of what she'd done to piss him off.

"Girl to be honest, he's mad for nothing really." She sucked her teeth and then went on to explain. "For the past month or so, he has been putting in a lot of overtime at work. I understand that we have a child and we need the money but by the time he comes home he's tired and doesn't have any energy to spend time with me or Korey for that matter. Most of the time, I've already put her to bed by the time that he comes in. He comes in, takes a shower, eats and goes straight to bed."

I wanted to slap the shit out of her for getting my hopes up for nothing! I'd thought that she was about to tell me that he was back up to his old bullshit, dealing with other bitches or something. Something that would give me some hope but instead here she was telling me about him working overtime and not spending enough time with her needy ass. Reflexively, I rolled my eyes up in my head at how petty she was.

"What?" She asked with her hand propped up on her hip.

"Huh?"

"Huh nothing, I saw that." She let me know wearing

a bothered expression. I hadn't been aware at the time that she'd seen my reaction but now I was well aware of the fact that she'd seen me. "Well...why did you roll your eyes up in your head?" She wanted to know.

I didn't bother looking up at her. Instead I busied myself with my client's hair. "Nelle..." I started. "Truthfully, I feel like you are being kind of petty and acting all needy. You are reminding me of Kisha a little bit." I teased laughing, hoping to lighten the mood a little because I could tell that I'd struck a nerve. I glanced over at her to see if she was laughing or if she'd even cracked a smile but I saw that she hadn't. "All I'm saying is, you have what you wanted, which was for Corey to stop running the streets and chasing bitches. He's not doing any of that anymore. That man worships the ground that you walk on and here you are showing him that still isn't enough by getting upset with him for working overtime to provide for his family. Shit like that is what pushes men back out into the streets."

"I am not saying that I don't appreciate the changes that he's made." She let out a frustrated breath and threw up her hands. "I'm just simply saying that he needs to have some balance. I am all for working and getting money but at the same time he needs to make time for his wife and child."

"I hear you and I get what you are saying but you may want to be a little careful of how you complain about it to him because he may feel like you are not fully seeing the effort that he is putting forth in trying to be the man that you wanted so desperately for him to be. He may be feeling like regardless of what he does you still have a complaint. That's just my opinion." Even though the shit I was telling her was some real shit, I honestly could've care less about her pathetic issues. I really hoped that all of her nagging and whining would push Corey away and right into another woman's bed, preferably mines.

"I appreciate your advice, Mina." She sounded

deflated. I knew how much she and Corey arguing affected her. I studied the sad expression on her face. She looked almost like she wanted to cry. I smiled inwardly at her misery.

"Y'all will be fine." I said trying to sound sincere. I finished with my client's hair and then got started on my next client. The rest of the day seemed to drag by and Nelle was no company at all. Talking about her and Corey's issues had killed the chipper mood that she'd been in earlier. A few times, I tried to get her to talk but not because I was trying to make her feel better but because I was bored. It didn't work though. She was too in her feelings. I started thinking to myself that maybe it was time to hire a few new people. Things weren't like they were before when I'd first opened the salon. Back then, Nelle, Mia and I got a long and we used to have so much fun at work together. Now, I only tolerated Nelle because she had no idea that I really didn't care to be around her at all. And Mia...well to be honest, the two of us were pretty cool until she decided to stick her nose where it didn't belong. In my opinion, she shouldn't have been concerned about me lusting after Corey. Her only concern should've been Ron but she and Nelle had always been the tightest of us three so I guess she felt like she was doing the right thing by calling herself checking me about Corey.

At the end of the day, Nelle and I cleaned up the shop in silence. The only noise that could be heard was the constant back to back ringing of my phone, which was starting to annoy me because Mello had been calling me back to back almost the entire evening. I didn't feel like being bothered with him. He knew that I was at work and that Simya was nowhere around. I felt like the only time that he and I needed to speak was when it concerned her. I wasn't about to spend precious time on the phone with him chopping it up like shit was sweet between us because it wasn't. He hadn't ever wanted to talk to me before he'd gotten locked up or when we were together. He'd never had the decency to sit and talk. All he'd wanted to do was argue and fight. So why should I waste my time on the phone talking to him? I'd made up my mind that we were done completely and there would be no more chances. I liked having my freedom and being able to live my life without all of the constant physical and verbal abuse. No one should have to live that way and I wasn't about to live that way anymore.

When Nelle and I were done, I locked up and headed to Tre's house. On my way, I smoked a half blunt that I'd left in my ashtray that morning. I knew that I was going to need something in order to deal with those crying ass babies of his. Lala had made a mess of them. They were way too spoiled. All they did was cry...like their whiny ass mama. I knew that my nerves couldn't take it. So I decided to prepare myself before I got there. When I'd finished smoking, I rolled down the window in an attempt to air out my hair and clothes. Then I cleaned my hands with hand sanitizer. I didn't want Tre to smell the scent of weed on me because that would definitely start an argument and I didn't feel like arguing with him.

I arrived at his house and noticed Kisha's car parked in the driveway. "Seriously?" I asked aloud, rolling my eyes and turning off the ignition. "What in the fuck is this nearly crippled bitch doing here?" I got out of the car and hit the door lock on my keychain. I held my keys in my hand as I made my way to the door, fingering the pepper spray that was attached to my keychain. Kisha and I hadn't been in the same space much since I'd been seeing Tre but I knew that she didn't really care for me and that she was feeling some kind of way about my being with him. Though she hadn't said anything to me directly, she'd said things to other people in town, who'd come right back to me and told every word that she'd said. She didn't have to like me or the fact that I was with Tre but if she tried to jump stupid I was going to empty the contents of the can that I was holding onto in her damn face.

I rang the bell and waited. After a few seconds, I heard someone unlocking the door. The door opened and Tre was standing on the other side wearing a pair of black basketball shorts and a black wifebeater, holding one of the babies in his arms.

"Hey, come on in." He invited me. His face held an agitated expression. He didn't wait for me to come in before turning and heading in the direction of the living room.

Lord please, don't *let me be walking in on some bullshit.* I thought to myself. All it would take was for him and Kisha to be having some sort of disagreement and then for her to see me walk in. I knew without a doubt shit would turn ugly really fast. I felt my heart rate speed up just thinking about it all. I walked in closing the door behind me and then followed him into the living room. The boys were running back and forth down the hallway playing, and the other baby was on the floor playing on a play mat. Kisha was sitting on the loveseat wearing a pink sweat suit and sporting a cute little short hairstyle. I noticed a pair of crutches propped up against the wall next to where she sat. From what Tre had told me, she had recovered really well from the accident that she and Skeet were in but she was still on crutches because her leg that had been broken hadn't completely healed. When she saw me she turned her nose up running her hand over her hair as if she were royalty or something. Tre took a seat on sofa across from Kisha and I sat on the other end down from him.

"Hey." I spoke nervously shifting my eyes, afraid to look directly at her. I didn't really want to speak but I was afraid that if I didn't she would think I was trying to be funny.

She looked me up and down and then rolled her eyes so hard that I thought for sure they would get stuck. I knew then speaking had been the wrong move. I gripped the pepper spray a little bit tighter. I was so nervous by now that my hands had begun to sweat.

"Hmph...I see the trash has arrived." She snapped still eyeing me, now looking me directly in my face. The look that she was giving me told me that she was totally disgusted by my presence. "I can't believe you have the nerve to come up in here talking about some damn 'hey'. Girl bye! Don't even play me like that."

"Kisha..." Tre interjected before I could respond and I was glad. "Chill out. I don't feel like no drama today."

"Oh, I'm good. I'll chill but she's not going to be walking up in here speaking to me like shit is sweet. Hell no, uh-uhh. That right there ain't gone work." She crossed her good leg over the broken one all dramatic, wagging her finger from side to side.

"Damn, she was just being polite." Tre continued to try and defuse the situation. "Must you always act a fool? And can you please watch your mouth around the kids?"

"If she wanted to be polite then she wouldn't have started fucking my babydaddy. A polite bitch would've said, 'nah I'll pass on that dick because it's attached to my cousin's babydaddy' but this thirsty hoe was all for fucking behind me!" She retorted sitting up on the edge of her seat. "Trust me...polite is the last thing she's trying to be."

"Maybe, I should leave." I suggested already standing.

"Nah, I invited you over here." Tre said. "Sit back down." I eased back down in the spot that I'd been sitting in, trying not to look at Kisha but I could feel her eyes still trained on me. "You're good." He looked at Kisha. "I'm not going to ask you again to chill out."

"Whatever." She snapped reaching next to the chair and grabbing her bag. She threw her bag on her shoulder before standing to her feet. She reached for her crutches and positioned them beneath her arms and then looked at Tre. "This is the reason why you and I don't get along because you don't see anything wrong with this picture right here. Then you have the audacity to sit up in here for the past thirty minutes or so and complain to me about Lala and the bad decision that she made. First of all, I don't see how you could even feel comfortable enough to talk to me about your problems with Lala being that she is the woman who you not only cheated on me with but also got pregnant, with not one but two babies. Nigga you've got a lot of nerve. When you do wrong shit you can't see it and when you do see it, you want everyone to be understanding and forgiving. Yet you aren't willing to give everyone else the same courtesy." She shook her head. "Tre, you are dead wrong. You really need to get your shit together, point blank period."

"What she did makes the shit that I've done look like nothing. So you can miss me with that bullshit!" He barked rising to his feet. The baby looked like she was scared to death as she held on tightly to Tre's shirt looking from him to Kisha.

"Really? You really believe that?" She asked not

backing down. "I am not and never will I ever be team Lala but I am a woman and a mother and I truly believe that girl had no idea that man would do anything to hurt those babies. She made a mistake. She trusted someone that she cared about!" She paused cocking her head to the side slightly with her lips pursed and looking at him clearly implying that she was making a point. "That isn't uncommon at all."

"Kisha please leave because if you don't, I won't be responsible for what I do to you!" Tre threatened. "Take Lola, Mina." He told me while practically throwing her onto my lap.

"I hope that you don't think you are scaring me." Kisha stood still looking up at him. He was now standing directly in her face. I sat only a few feet from them, wondering if I should toss Lola's little ass on the sofa and roll out or if I should stay put. I truly had no idea what to do. All of the chaos had managed to blow my high.

"I'm not trying to scare you. You just need to leave

because you've gotten on my damn nerves and I am trying my best not to lay hands on you."

"I'd advise you not to do that." She told him calmly. "I am not going to stand here and bite my tongue because you don't like what I am saying. I haven't said anything wrong. Everything that has come out of my mouth has been right, from the way I feel about that little hoe..." She looked around him and pointed at me. "To the way I feel about how you are carrying shit in this situation with Lala. You are wrong Tre. You know for a fact that I would never take up for that girl but right is right. That girl has kept my children and never did anything wrong to them. She actually took damn good care of them when she was here and they would come over. Hell, they had fallen in love with her. So yes, I feel like you are wrong for taking those babies from her."

"I don't give a fuck what you think! I asked you to get the fuck out!" He exploded pushing her really hard. She fell back onto the loveseat, her crutches falling onto the floor next to the chair. I wanted to get up and run but I was paralyzed by fear. I couldn't believe that he'd pushed her with her being on crutches but he obviously didn't give a damn. As I sat there looking at the shocked expression on Kisha's face, I realized that she hadn't thought that he would put his hands on her either.

That's what your mouthy ass get! I laughed in my head. *That mouth of yours got your half crippled ass in trouble. Bet you will shut up now.* I prayed that she wasn't thinking I was going to get up and help her after how she'd been treating me ever since I'd walked in the door. He could beat the dog shit out of her and break her other leg for all I cared!

The boys came running into the living room. "Daddy, stop fighting!" One of them yelled.

"Everything is alright boys." Kisha spoke from where she'd landed on the loveseat. Though her voice was calm, her expression told that she was pissed. "Go back down the hall to your room and play." They looked from her to Tre but didn't budge. "Go ahead." She urged. After a few seconds, reluctantly they turned and left the room but I could tell that they didn't want to.

Tre stood over Kisha with his chest heaving up and down, staring down at her through angry eyes. "Leave Kisha…" He repeated in a much calmer voice. He bent down and picked up her crutches propping them against the loveseat.

She stood up, repositioned her crutches beneath her arms and then picked up her bag again which had fallen off her shoulder when he'd pushed her back onto the loveseat. "I'm going to allow you to have that one push but please let that be your last…okay?" She told him the clenched teeth. "You screaming that you don't give a fuck what I think but if I remember correctly, before that tramp walked in you were asking me what I thought of the situation! So now I am telling you! What makes your parenting any better than Lala's or anyone else's for that matter. You aren't any better, Tre. You have an outside bitch in here around your babies now. Who's to say that she wouldn't do anything to hurt them? You allowed Lala around my kids, knowing that she and I don't like each other. She could've done something to them out of spite, you had no idea but you trusted her around them, assuming that she wouldn't harm them. That is the same exact thing that she did. It's just that the person whom she trusted turned out to be a sorry piece of shit. If you want to place blame, place blame on the sorry motherfucka who actually tried to harm your baby, not that child's mother because you know deep down in your heart that girl loves those kids. And another thing, do you really feel like you are not hurting them by snatching them away from her. Those kids are used to waking up every day to her...not you but her." She shook her head again. "Tre, you need to think about this shit because it ain't right. Talking about you called Mina over here do their hair. Call their damn mama and stop acting stupid!"

"Are you done yet?" He asked her.

"Nah, I'm not done yet. You're standing up here calling out everybody else's flaws. Yet every time I turn around you are putting your hands on me. What kind of father are you?" She asked. "Are you teaching your sons that it's okay to beat on women?"

"You started this shit, not me." He corrected her. "And I didn't hit you! I pushed you."

"Whatever...it's the same damn thing. Every time you get upset you feel like it's okay to put your hands on me. Just think about the message you are sending to your kids...Father of the Year." She taunted. "Now, I'm done."

"Good."

She yelled down the hallway and told the boys to come on. They both came running. After they'd both given Tre a hug and kiss. He told them he'd call them later and they left.

Mina

Once Kisha and the boys were gone, I placed Lola on the play mat next to Laila. No sooner than her ass touched the floor she started to cry. I rolled my eyes up in my head and quickly scooped her back up. I didn't want her crying to cause Tre to become more upset than he already was. He'd disappeared down the hallway in one of the back rooms.

"Ughh...will you shut up that damn crying please?" I mumbled to Lola as I shook her. She looked up at me still sniffling but no longer crying, her little head bobbling back and forth. I tried placing her on the floor again and she started to cry before I got her halfway down. I placed her back on my lap. "Shut the hell up! I am not about to sit here and hold your little ass." I gritted pinching her leg. She let out a loud squeal. I smirked, thinking to myself, *now you have a reason to cry with your spoiled little ass!*

"What in the world is wrong with my baby?" Tre asked nearly running back down the hall with an unlit cigarette stuck between his lips.

I snuggled Lola against my chest and rocked her back and forth. "She's crying because I tried to put her down on the floor with Laila. She wants to be held." I half lied because that was part of the reason why she was crying.

"Awww...come here princess." He said in a baby-like voice as he came over and took her from my lap. "She's probably sleepy." He took the cigarette from between his lips and laid it on the coffee table.

"Yeah, she probably is." I agreed dryly. "Where is a

comb so that I can start on Laila's hair?"

"There's a comb in the bedroom on the dresser." He replied. He was now sitting on the loveseat with Lola lying on his chest. She was sucking her finger, still sniffling and staring at me like I was some evil monster.

That's right. Get a good look so you will know that I am not the bitch to play with. I do not like spoiled ass kids. Especially one's that I didn't push out of my fuckin' womb. I said in my head staring back at her, still wearing a smirk.

I got up and went down the hall and retrieved the comb and a jar of hair grease from the bathroom. I went back into the living room and picked Laila up from the floor. She started kicking and screaming as soon as I picked her up. *Ain't this about a bitch!* I was beyond annoyed.

"Laila chill out." Tre told her. She got quiet for a second and then started back throwing a tantrum. He got up and picked some toys up from the floor and gave them to her. "Here you go. Now shut that fuss up." She immediately got quiet.

I got started on her hair, all the while I couldn't stop thinking about the things that Kisha had said to Tre before she'd left. I wanted to know exactly what Lala's boyfriend had done to one of the girl's that had caused Tre to take them from her.

I looked over at him, he had his eyes closed and was slowly rocking Lola from side to side. She had her eyes closed as well, proving that he'd been right about her being sleepy. I decided this would be the best time to put on my concerned girlfriend act so that I could find out what had happened.

"Bae, are you alright?" I asked.

"Yeah, I guess." He said with a sigh, still not opening his eyes.

"What's going on? Maybe I can help."

""Thanks but I doubt if you can help."

"You won't know unless you tell me."

He opened his eyes and looked over at me. "Shit is

just all fucked up." He started. "This nigga that Lala was fuckin' touched Lola. Luckily, Lala walked in before he had a chance to actually do anything else to her besides touch her..."

My mouth fell wide open. I couldn't believe the shit that I'd just heard. "Hold up, wait a minute." I interrupted. I needed to be sure that he'd just said what I'd thought he'd said. That wasn't at all what I'd been expecting. "What do you mean, he touched the baby? Touched her how? Like down there?" I pointed down between my legs. He nodded his head. The pain in his eyes and in his expression told me that talking about this was hard for him but I didn't care. I wanted to know everything, every single detail. This was much juicer than anything I could've ever imagined. Nelle's mouth was going to hit the floor when I told her about this. "Oh my God, that sick bastard." Even though, I was being nosey and wanted to know all of the details, I truly did feel bad about what had happened to Lola. Hearing this almost made me regret shaking and pinching her but then again she had deserved that. No child deserved to be sexually assaulted in anyway by anyone.

"Yeah, Lala had left them with him while she made a quick run to the grocery store but on her way to the store, she realized that she'd left her pocketbook and went back to the house. She used her key to let herself in and that's when she saw him with his pants down jacking off and rubbing on Lola."

A visual of that sick scene popped into my head and I nearly gagged. My phone started to vibrate serving as a momentary distraction. I picked it up and looked at it seeing that I had a text message. I opened up the message and saw that it was from Mello asking me to give him a call. I smacked my lips and closed the message. I was sick of him blowing up my phone. Me not answering his calls should've told him that I wasn't interested in talking to him. *How in the fuck do these niggas be getting cell phones in jail anyways?* I wondered to myself before powering my phone off and laying it back down on the arm of the sofa. I focused my attention back on Tre, reaching over and gently caressing his leg.

"I'm sorry to hear what dude did to Lola. There is no excuse for a grown ass man to be touching on a baby." I honestly meant that. I hoped that whoever this guy was who'd done that sick shit was beneath the jail. "I can totally understand why you are upset. I would be ready to kill someone if a nigga did some shit like that to Simya." I shook my head at the horrible thought and at the same time an uneasy feeling washed over me.

Tre rubbed Lola's back and kissed her on top of her head. "Trust me, he would be a dead man if they hadn't locked his ass up before I arrived." He assured me. "Kisha seems to think that I am wrong for taking my babies away from Lala's irresponsible ass. She can say what she wants but I did what I felt needed to be done to ensure that no more bullshit like this happens again. Lala is lucky that's all I did was take my kids from her stupid ass." He looked as if he was starting to get heated all over again.

As much as I didn't want to further upset him, I was 100% with Kisha about him shipping those two whining ass babies back to their mama. I wasn't about to be playing stepmama to their little asses. I hadn't signed up for that shit and there was no way he was about to just force it upon me. I only had one child for a reason, because I didn't want anymore.

"Tre, I know that Lala made a bad decision by leaving the girls with her boyfriend but I honestly don't believe she knew he would do anything to harm them. I bet she is more upset with herself than you could ever be." I started slowly, praying silently that he didn't flip out and beat the hell out of me. So far he was just sitting on the other end of the chair, still rubbing Lola's back and looking in the other direction. I took a deep breath and continued, "I don't know Lala but I can tell by the way she's always calling you bragging about the latest achievements of those girls that she really loves them a lot. Anyone can see that she takes damn good care of them. Try and put your anger to the side for a minute, just a minute and look at the entire picture and not just this situation. Has she ever mistreated your daughters before or given you any reason to question her as a parent?" I couldn't tell if he was listening to me or not because he hadn't said anything or even bothered to look in my direction. I decided to let what I'd said sink in before saying anything more. Plus, I didn't want to say too much and get the wrong reaction.

I finished Laila's last braid and then picked her up. She looked like she was getting sleepy. She was rubbing her eyes and sucking on her two middle fingers. I took her down the hall, changed her pamper and laid her in her crib. I was surprised when she didn't start to cry but relieved that she didn't. I went back into the living room and sat back down in my same spot.

"Tre give me the baby so that I can do her hair real

quick." I told him. I was starting to feel the effects of being up since 6:00am that morning and standing on my feet all day. My body was tired, fingers were starting to cramp and I was getting a little sleepy. All I wanted was to do Lola's hair, go home, take a shower and go to bed.

"Won't that wake her?" He asked looking down at her.

"Nah, that's the only time that I can do Simya's hair, is when she's asleep." I laughed taking Lola from his arms and laying her across my lap.

He got up and left the room disappearing down the hallway again. He returned a few seconds later puffing on a cigarette. I could tell that he had a lot on his mind because he'd forgotten all about the cigarette that he'd placed on the coffee table. "Yo, do you want something to drink?" He asked and then named off my choices. "I have some Pepsi, some water and some Kool-Aid."

"I'll take the Pepsi." I replied as I started to braid Lola's hair. Tre went into the kitchen and came back with two cans of Pepsi. He handed one to me and popped the top on the other one, taking a sip before sitting down. "Thank you." I opened mine and took a few sips before placing it on the coffee table and continuing Lola's hair.

"Maybe, Lala didn't mean for this to happen but I still can't allow her to take my babies back to Danville. I just can't do that." He shook his head and then took a pull of his cigarette. He held his head in his hands. "I can't trust her judgment right now."

"I understand that and I am not saying that you are wrong for that because you are not. You are protecting your babies, which is what you should be doing but at the same time you have to think about how what you are doing is affecting them as well. They are not used to being away from their mama, Tre." I paused. "You and Lala need to talk. Give her a chance to talk and explain her side of things. I can see that you are hurting and I am willing to bet that she is too." I was so proud of myself because I could tell my little fake speech and concerned act was working. I could almost see Lala in the driveway loading up her little brats to take their asses back up the road!

Tre lifted his head from his hands and took a pull of his cigarette. "I need some time before I can talk to her. Right now I am too upset."

"I feel you." I finished up Lola's hair and then Tre put her to bed.

I was in the bathroom washing my hands, when Tre walked in and slipped his arms around my waist. The gesture kind of took me by surprise because we really hadn't been on that level in a minute. He moved my hair out of the way and kissed my neck. "I'm sorry that I haven't been able to give our relationship the attention that it deserves. I've thought about some of the things that you've been complaining about and I realize that I do tend to overdo it a bit when it comes to Kisha and Lala. I guess I would feel some kind of way if the tables were turned and you were always running whenever your babydaddy called." He explained. I didn't say anything I just rested my head back against his chest and listened. "I just be trying to do what I feel is right. I have made so many mistakes in the past and done so much wrong by both of my babymamas that I am constantly trying to make it up to them and to my kids. So in my eyes it makes sense to jump and run every time one of them calls but I can see now after taking a step back why it doesn't make sense to you. I guess in trying so hard to do right by them and be there for them and my kids, I forgot all about you and our relationship. That's not what I'm trying to do. I want to try and make this work, if that's still what you want." He kissed my neck again, looking up in the mirror and waiting for me to reply.

I should've been honest with him at that moment and told him the truth. That I was so fucked up on the inside, I really had no idea what I wanted. Some days, I really did feel like I wanted to be with him. Overall, he was a decent man. He'd been helping to take care of my daughter ever since we'd started seeing each other. He gave me money, helped out with my bills even though he hardly ever stayed at my place, and he'd never put his hands on me. For me, that was definitely a come up in the relationship department. Not to mention that the sex was some of the best I'd ever had. I knew that I should be satisfied with him but I wasn't. I couldn't be even if I wanted to because no matter how hard I tried I couldn't shake the desire that I had to be with Corey. I couldn't be honest with Tre though because there was no way I was about to give up his money, the things that he did for my daughter or his dick. He was more like a father to Simya than Mello had ever been. If I told him the truth, I knew that he wouldn't continue to stick around and be there for Simya. He would be a fool to. So I kept my truth to myself and continued to do what I did best...played along.

"Of course, I still want this to work." I lied.

"Good." He turned me around so that I was facing

him and then lifted me up on the sink. Positioning himself between my legs he leaned down and kissed me, slipping his tongue inside my mouth. I kissed him back sucking on his tongue and running my hands over his chest. I felt the spot between my legs become moist and my clit start to throb.

He broke our kiss. "Let's take this to the bedroom." He breathed huskily against my lips and then kissed me again. I wrapped my arms around his neck and my legs around his waist. We continued to kiss as he carried me down the hall to the bedroom. Once we were inside the bedroom he pushed the door closed with his foot and carried me over to the bed. He put me down next to the bed. I hurriedly undressed while he did the same. It'd been a while since the two of us were intimate and I couldn't wait to feel his tongue dancing over my clit. He was blessed in the dick department but nothing could compare to that hurricane tongue of his. Just thinking about it made me damn near rip my panties in half trying to get them off. I threw them next to the rest of my clothes that were in a pile on the floor next to my feet. Then I sat down on the bed and scooted to the middle of it staring up at Tre but in my mind he wasn't who I was seeing...I was seeing Corey. Hell they always said if you can't love the one you want, love the one you're with...and just imagine that it's the one you want. He was completely naked now standing there looking like a chocolate God stroking his massive erection and looking at me like he was about to do some serious damage to my kitty kat. I bit down on my bottom lip seductively and crooked my index finger at him.

"Come to mama, baby." I whispered in a sultry voice. "Come here and let me help you relieve some of that pent up frustration."

He crawled on the bed pushing me back roughly, I giggled as he took both of my legs and pushed them back as far as they would go before burying his face in my pussy. He devoured me like I was his last meal and got me off twice before coming up for air. As I lay there in the middle of his bed, body covered in sweat and trembling. He planted kisses all over my stomach, my neck, my chin and then finally he reached my lips.

"You good, Lil Bit?" He asked between kisses.

I had my eyes squeezed shut and I didn't bother to open them because I didn't want to mess up my fantasy by seeing his face. "Yes baby, I'm good." I answered in my mind I was staring up into Corey's eyes with my fingers entangled in his dreads. I felt the head of Tre's swollen member at my opening and then he was sliding inside of me. I gripped the covers tightly and thrust my hips upward to meet his strokes. He licked and sucked on my neck and ears increasing the pleasure and bringing me closer to my next orgasm. He strokes became faster and deeper. Sweat dripped from the both of us as we went at it almost like animals at this point. He pulled out of me and flipped me over like I didn't weight more than a couple of pounds. With my head down, face in the pillow and ass tooted up in the air, I braced myself. Tre gripped my hips and plunged into me as far as he could go. I threw the pussy back at him daring him to go harder and he did. The only sounds that could be heard were our moans, heavy breathing, the constant slapping of skin and the headboard banging against the wall. It didn't take long for us both to reach our climax.

Tre collapsed next to me and then pulled me into his arms. He moved my hair back out of my face and kissed me on my forehead. "Damn, I needed that."

"Me too." I replied with a lazy smile playing on my lips. I finally opened my eyes and looked over at Tre, my smile fading because he wasn't who I wanted him to be. "I need to get up so that I can take my butt home."

"Home?" He looked confused.

"Yeah...home." I said sitting up. "I need to go pick up my child and go home."

"Mina, do you see what time it is?" He asked sitting up and turning on the lamp. "It's almost 10:00. I am sure that your mama has put Simya to bed. You may as well just stay here."

By now, I was standing next to the bed pulling my shirt on. "Simya is more than likely still up playing." I told him, knowing that my mama had Simya in bed hours ago. "Besides if I go home, I don't have to worry about getting up twenty minutes early so that I can drive home and get dressed. I will already be there."

"Alright." He threw up his hands.

"Don't be mad baby. I will stay with you another night."

"Yeah...that's cool."

I could tell by his tone that he wasn't pleased but I really didn't care. "Are you going to walk me to the door?" I asked once I was done getting dressed.

He got up, put on his boxers and then looked at me and asked. "You ready?"

"Yeah..." He led the way and I followed him down the hall. In the living room, I gathered my pocketbook, phone and keys. He walked with me outside to my car and held the door for me to get inside. I tossed my bag inside and then gave him a quick peck on the lips. "I'll call you when I get home to let you know that I made it safely."

"Cool..." Was his reply.

"Tre...don't act like that. I told you why I can't stay."

"Okay, we're good. I'm not mad...I wish that you could stay but...I understand that you need to go and pick up your baby." He gave me another quick peck. "Don't forget to call me."

"Okay, I won't." I got in my car and backed out of the driveway. I wasn't down the road a mile before I reached over and took my cell out of my pocketbook and powered it on. As soon as it came on, two text messages came through and my voicemail notification alerted me that I had a new voicemail. I checked the texts and they were both from Mello still asking me to give him a call and asking me why was I ignoring him. I rolled my eyes up in my head before going to my contacts and finding Nelle's name. I pressed her name and waited for the call to connect. The phone rang a few times before, she picked up sounding upset.

"Hey." She answered.

"Hey girl, are you okay?" I asked trying my best to sound concerned.

"Hell nah, I'm not alright." She snapped. "It's going on 11:00 in the damn night and Corey hasn't made it home yet!" I heard her voice crack. "I am getting tired now and I don't want to hear any more bullshit about he's working late! My gut is telling me that he's up to no damn good!"

"I feel you cuz but try to calm down." I smiled wanting to burst out laughing. "You may be getting yourself all worked up for nothing. I doubt if Corey is silly enough to be back up to his old bullshit. He has worked too hard to prove to you that he wasn't like that anymore. Just try and give him the benefit of the doubt before you go jumping the gun."

"Fuck that! I have..." Her words trailed off and then I heard her asking, "Where have you been?" I knew then that Corey had just walked in. I heard him saying something but I couldn't make out what it was. The next thing I heard was Nelle going off. I pressed end and disconnected the call.

"Guess, I know who won't be getting any dick tonight." I laughed aloud. "There seems to be a bit of trouble in paradise."

Kisha

A few days after the incident with Tre, I found myself standing on Skeet's front porch just before noon. I'd been standing there debating whether or not to ring the bell. I wasn't sure if going to his place had been a smart decision. He'd been begging me for weeks to come over so that we could talk, saying that he had some things that he needed to say to me face to face and up until that morning I'd been refusing to see him or speak to him. I was angry with him for nearly taking my life as well as his own in the car accident. For some reason, maybe stupidity, after hearing how pitiful he'd sounded on the voicemail he'd left early that morning, I'd broken down and went to see what he wanted. I figured that it couldn't hurt to at least hear him out. I would've made him come to me but he couldn't because he was still recovering from the two broken legs that he'd suffered from the car accident.

I rang the doorbell and waited, looking out across the yard at the neighbors in the yard next door. The man was outside playing football with his two boys while his wife stood on the porch and watched. I felt a pang of jealousy. I wished that could've been Tre and I. I wished that things had turned out differently instead of the way that they were now. I'd never wanted for my children to grow up in a broken home. I'd wanted to give them what I never had, a mother and a father. I'd done all that I could to ensure that but it still hadn't been enough. Being young and dumb, I'd never stopped to think that in order for a relationship to work both people involved had to want the same thing and work towards that. Instead I'd thought that if I loved Tre enough and put up with all of his bullshit, eventually he'd chose his family over the hoes in the streets. I shook my head at the realization of how stupid I'd been. I continued to watch the family next door until my attention was pulled away by the sound of the door being unlocked.

The door opened and Skeet sat in a wheelchair. He looked the same except he'd cut his beard and there were a few scars along the side of his face that I assume were a result of the accident. I stood there momentarily frozen just staring at him. I'd thought that my first time seeing him I would be upset and curse him lower than a dog for how he'd put both of our lives in danger. I thought that all of the anger that had been pent up inside of me for the past two and a half months would surely would surely boil over and I'd explode but for some reason the opposite of that was happening. I felt bad seeing him in the condition that he was in. The Skeet that I knew had always exuded strength but this man sitting before me didn't exude that at all. Instead he looked weak and fragile and a part of me felt that I was partially the blame. It was like a wave of emotion hit me as soon as he opened the door. In my mind, I kept seeing the sad, upset expression that he'd worn in the doctor's office the day of the accident. I saw the pain in his eyes when I'd told him only days before that I didn't plan on keeping his baby. I felt bad now as those images played back in my mind. I wished that I could have a chance to do it all over again. I would've handled it differently. I would've broken the news to him in a better way instead of being as insensitive as I had. At the time I hadn't really taken the time to consider his feelings at all. I'd only been thinking of my own.

"Hey, come in." He spoke moving back out of the way of the door so that I could get past him. I walked in closing the door behind me. "We can go into the kitchen. I was eating some lunch. Are you hungry?"

"Nah, I'm good." I replied trailing him into the kitchen. I took a seat at the table across from where he had a plate that held a sandwich and some chips sitting.

"Are you sure that you don't want any?" He offered again as he positioned his chair at the table. "You know how I get down in the kitchen so you know it's good." He cracked a slight smile revealing deep dimples in each of his cheeks. It'd been years since I'd seen those dimples because they'd been hidden by the full beard that he'd been sporting.

"I don't want anything to eat." I said wanting to get to the point of my visit. I didn't like the affect that he was having on me. I'd been doing a lot of thinking over the past couple of months about changes that I wanted to make within my life for myself and my boys they didn't include a man. It was time for me to focus on being a mother and establishing some type of stability for my boys and for myself. I was getting older not younger. For years, I'd been depending on Tre and my family to take care of me and the boys. I'd even depended on Skeet at one point in time. I didn't want to depend on anybody else anymore. It was time for me to depend on me and that is exactly what I was about to do as soon as I was able to get around without the crutches that I was using. "What did you need me to come by for?"

I watched closely as the smile faded from his face and was replaced by a serious expression. He took a sip from the glass of juice that was sitting on the table and then placed it back down next to the plate and took a deep breath. "Kish...I'm sorry for everything."

I interrupted him because I didn't feel that it was necessary for him to keep on apologizing over and over. "Skeet, you've already apologized a million times through text and on my voicemail."

"I know that but I wanted to say it to you...face to face." He let me know. "Can I finish, please?"

"Yeah..."

"Like I was saying, I am sorry for everything that happened. I am especially sorry about the accident. Every time that I think about it, it nearly kills me thinking of what could have happened. Not what could've happened to me but what could've happened to you, you could've died that day." He looked up at me and I saw tears in his eyes. He shook his head and ran his hand over his face. "I don't think I could've lived with myself knowing that I'd been the cause of your death. I would've taken my own life."

"Skeet, it wasn't all your fault." I said after seeing how upset he was. I could see that he really was sorry and it touched me. "I could've handled things differently than I did that day. It was my insensitiveness that cause you to lose it the way that you did. I never took the time to think about how my decision would affect you. At the time, I didn't care to be honest. I was only thinking about myself and the fact that I didn't want another child. I should've known that you would be upset but like I said at that time I didn't care."

"Yeah but I still had no right to put my hands on you. No matter how upset I was. That was no excuse." We both got quiet for a moment and then he continued. "I have never loved a woman like I love you. I've loved you for a very long time now. I can remember seeing you with Tre and wishing that you were mine before anything ever happened between us. I've always felt like he didn't deserve you because of all of the things that I knew that he was doing out in the streets. I would always say to myself that if given the chance, I could make you happier and treat you like you deserved to be treated. Then when I finally got that chance, I nearly killed you." He let out a sarcastic chuckle.

"Skeet will you stop talking like you did it on purpose. It was a mistake."

"Nah, I allowed my anger and pain to cloud my better judgment. I was so mad at you for wanting to have an abortion that I didn't take the time to think about what might happen if we started fighting in that car while I was driving."

"I guess we both used bad judgment."

"Yeah…I guess we did."

He looked over at me and asked. "Can I ask you something?"

I wasn't sure if I should say yes but I nodded my head anyways.

"Why didn't you want my baby? I mean, what made my baby any different from Shaun and Quan? Was it because it wasn't Tre's? I need to know because that has been fucking with me since the night that you told me that you thought that you were pregnant and didn't want to keep it."

"I didn't need another child…we didn't need a child together."

He looked confused. "What? What is that supposed to mean? And why is that something that you felt like you were the only one who had a right to decide? If I remember correctly, it takes two people to lie down and create a life. So how come, only one gets to decide to end it?"

I let out a frustrated breath. "Skeet, us being together in the first place was a mistake." I saw a pained expression take over his face. So I explained. "I should never have left Tre and ran directly to your bed. That was the wrong way for me to handle the pain that he'd caused me. I didn't want to deal with it at that time, I wanted something to numb it, something to take my mind off of it and that something was you. You were my distraction and at the same time you were my payback. I knew that being with you would hurt Tre and that's exactly what I wanted. I wanted to hurt him the same way that he'd hurt me by sleeping with all of those other women out in the streets and getting Lala pregnant. I wanted to show him that he wasn't the only one who could do some foul shit because I knew that he'd never expect me to fuck with someone else. Especially not one of his boys."

"Wooow...really? Is that really how you felt about me? That I was just some gotdamn rebound!" He roared. I'd known that my words wouldn't be easy for him to hear but they were the truth.

"Skeet..."

"Skeet my ass, Kish!" He banged his fist on the arm of the chair, cutting me off. I was kind of glad that he was in a wheelchair because if he hadn't been there's no telling what he may have done to me in that kitchen. "Was I just something for you to do the first time that we fucked too? Was I just something to numb your pain then too?"

"Yeah..." I lowered my eyes feeling guilty because I'd always known how deeply that he cared for me. I'd never meant to hurt him but clearly I had.

He backed his chair away from the table and rolled towards the living room. I got up and followed him. I didn't bother grabbing my crutches. "Just leave me alone, yo. On some real shit, you can leave because I really don't even want to look at you right now. I've said everything that I wanted to say as far as me being sorry about the accident."

"Skeet, what more did you expect? Did you honestly think that I was over Tre that quickly? Did you really think that I was in love with you or that I could be so soon after everything that had just happened between Tre and me?" I yelled after him, limping as quickly as my one good leg would carry me while trying not to put any pressure on my bad leg. "I'm not saying that I was right for how I handled the situation but stop acting like you were some clueless victim! You knew what time it was! You knew all the while how I felt about Tre and so you had to know that all of those feelings hadn't just vanished overnight!"

He stopped and swirled his chair around to face me! "I also knew how you still kept in contact with me after the first time we fucked! How whenever we were in the same space together you would flirt with me on the low. You led me to believe that even though you were too weak to pick up and leave Tre, that you did have some kind of feelings for me deep down inside! I'm not saying that I thought that your feelings for him had all vanished but I did think that once you found out about his other family you were done and ready to move on. Ready to begin a new chapter of your life with me and finally give us a real chance because you knew that is what I wanted. You knew that because I constantly told you that! So how about you stop acting as if you didn't know what fuckin' time it was! You knew but your selfish ass didn't care!"

I stood there with my mouth opened wide, shocked by the last words that he'd said. I threw up my hands. "You know what, I am not about to stand here and argue with you about who was right and who was wrong about how things began and ended between us. "We" are a thing of the past. So there is really no need for us to be going back and forth."

"I'll never understand how women will sit and complain about being with a motherfucka who treats them like shit, cheats and beats on them but when they find a good nigga that actually loves and cares for them they will do him fucked up." He looked me in my eyes. "I guess when you're used to being treated like shit. You start to think that is the way shit should be."

I didn't feel like arguing with him anymore. "Good bye Skeet." I told him turning and limping back into the kitchen to get my crutches.

"Fuck you, Kisha!" I heard him yell after me. I didn't reply I just kept walking. I was learning that sometimes it was best to keep your mouth shut and walk away.

Lala

I walked through the house one last time checking to see if I had everything and if I'd turned off all of the appliances and lights. I was leaving, headed to Boykins. It'd been a week and a half since I'd seen my babies and I couldn't stand not seeing them another day. The only reason that I'd waited so long was to try and allow Tre sometime to cool off because I didn't want to fight with him once I got there. I was hoping that the two of us could possibly sit down and try to figure out some way to co-parent without things having to get ugly. The last time that I'd seen him things had gotten really out of hand. I was still in disbelief about the whole gun situation. I knew that in my heart I would never be able to look at him in the same way ever again. I'd lost all respect for him that night because he'd shown me that he didn't have any at all for me. That had topped any and everything that he'd ever done in the past. Those things had been forgivable but him pulling a gun on me wasn't something that I could never forgive or forget for that matter. Regardless of how mad he'd been, he still should've never allowed his anger to push him to that point. Not only that but I felt like he should've known me better than to believe that I'd ever do anything to hurt my babies. Yes, I'd made a bad decision which had led to something awful happening but he couldn't hold me accountable for Reggie's actions. The Tre that I'd seen looking back at me that night standing in my hallway with a gun aimed at my face, wasn't the man that I'd fallen in love with. He wasn't the same man that I'd gone out of my way to protect and in the process given up everything and even left my home. He wasn't the man that I'd wanted so desperately to be with and raise my daughters with. He was someone else. It'd crossed my mind a million and one times since that night how he'd had the audacity to look down on me for not "knowing" Reggie but the truth was I really didn't know him either and he'd proven that time and time again through his actions. He'd done some really foul shit over the past year and a half that I would've never expected from him, leaving me wondering if it was really safe to say that I "knew" anybody. Maybe I, like everybody else, just thought I "knew" a lot of motherfuckas but in reality only knew what they chose to reveal.

I stopped in the hallway and leaned back against the wall for a few seconds. I took a deep breath and exhaled and then I repeated the same thing once more. For some reason, I'd been having this nervous feeling in the pit of my stomach since the day before and something in the back of my mind was telling me not to go to Boykins. Almost like God was trying to warn me about something but I had to go. There was no way I could continue on like this, not seeing my kids and not knowing how they were doing. I'd called numerous times to check on them but Tre ignored all of my calls. I'd thought about calling his mother and asking her how they were but I wasn't sure of what he'd told her about the situation and how she may have felt about me at this point. I was almost sure that after hearing Tre's version of what had happened she probably hated me too and felt that I was an unfit parent as well.

"Lord please take this feeling away. Whatever it is, I'm putting it in your hands." I looked upward in the direction of the ceiling and whispered before pulling myself together and going back into the living room.

"Do you have everything?" Nisey asked glancing back at me as I entered the room. She was closing the blinds. She'd demanded to ride with me to Boykins and had let me know that she wasn't taking no for an answer. She didn't trust Tre after how he'd showed out and I didn't either. With this bad feeling that I was having, I was kind of glad that she was going with me. Maybe her being there would help to ease my nerves some.

"Yeah, I believe that I do. Whatever I don't have, I guess will be fine." I said running my hand over my face. I was drained, both physically and mentally because I hadn't had much sleep since everything that had taken place. I didn't have any appetite at all. I missed my babies so bad that it hurt. They'd never been away from me for more than a couple hours. The past week and a half had been pure torture. The only good thing that had managed to happen was the judge had denied Reggie of a bond when he'd gone to court the week before. I was thankful for that. I hoped that they never let his no good ass out.

He'd had the nerve to try and apologize when he'd seen me. I'd turned and walked off. Fuck him and his apology, certain shit was unforgivable and fucking with my babies was definitely on the list!

Nisey and I walked out of the house and I locked the doors behind us.

"Do you want me to drive?" Nisey offered as we walked towards my car. "You don't look so good."

"I have a migraine." I admitted, choosing to leave out the part about the feeling that I was having. I'd taken two Aleve when I'd first woke but they hadn't helped at all. "All of this mess that's been going on has me stressed out something awful."

"I know it does but everything is going to be alright." She said sympathetically holding her hand out. "Give me the keys. I'll drive and you can try to relax and take a nap because you are going to need to be alert once you get to Boykins. Laila and Lola are going to wear your butt out!" She giggled. I knew that she was trying to cheer me up but it didn't work because all I kept thinking to myself was that Tre wasn't going to make things that easy for me. Knowing him, he was going to try and show his black ass when I showed up to get my babies but it was what it was because I wasn't leaving Boykins without my babies.

I gave her the keys and then walked around the car and opened up the door. I tried forcing a smile as I slid in on the passenger side. "Yeah...I hope so." I replied quietly as I sat my pocketbook down next to my feet and buckled my seatbelt. I propped my arm up against the door and rested my head against my hand.

Nisey got in on the other side and buckled her seatbelt as well. "You'll see. Those girls are going to be so happy to see you, you aren't going to be able to put them down." She started the car, put it in drive and drove out of the driveway.

I looked out the window and started to pray silently again. I felt like I couldn't pray enough. *Lord please don't let this trip end up being horrible. I just want to get my babies and bring them home. I don't want to deal with any drama from Tre, Kisha or his new girlfriend. I just want to get my babies and leave. I've dealt with enough drama and nonsense and my babies have been through enough as well. Please Lord, be in control of this situation and allow things to work out maturely and peacefully. Amen...*

I took a deep breath and let it out slowly. Normally saying a prayer always made me feel better but I'd been praying all night and all morning and nothing had changed. If anything it'd gotten worse. I just couldn't shake the bad feeling that I had in the pit of my stomach. I already knew that I was headed directly into some bullshit and the only thing that kept crossing my mind was the gun that Tre'd had that night at my house. The feeling that I had was so strong I damn near wanted to tell Nisey to turn around and let's not go but I had to see my girls so instead of saying anything, I kept quiet and continued to pray silently.

"What's on your mind?" Nisey inquired tearing me away from my thoughts. She reached over and turned down the radio, which had already been low to start with. Now it couldn't be heard at all. "You are all quiet over there staring out the window. What's up?"

"Nothing." I lied rubbing my temples. My migraine seemed to be getting worse. The pain had become almost unbearable. I reached down and picked up my pocketbook placing it on my lap. I took out the bottle of Aleve, opened them and shook two into my hand. I closed the bottle, placed it back in my bag and took the water that I'd bought out and used it to take the pills. When I was done, I placed my pocketbook back on the floor.

"Try to relax and take a nap Lala that will make your head feel better." Nisey said momentarily taking her eyes off of the road and glancing over at me. I could see concern written all over her face. "I know that a lot has happened over the past week and a half but you've still got to take care of yourself. Those two little girls need their mama because Tre and nobody else is going to take care of them or treat them like you do. You are a great mother and I don't give a damn what Tre, social services or nobody else says. I'm telling you that you are a damn good mother. You made a mistake, you misjudged Reggie's sorry ass but that doesn't make you unfit. It makes you human. We all make mistakes and the last time that I checked there weren't any perfect motherfuckas walking around here. So you quit all of that worrying and stressing and pull it together for them babies so that you will be feeling good enough to play with them and spoil them when you get down there. Fuck Tre and if he want to get stupid, we can do that too. We will turn Boykins out down here today!"

Hearing how she had my back brought a proud smile to my face and actually managed to ease my nerves a little. "Girl, you are a mess." I laughed.

She laughed too. "Nah, I just don't like seeing you

like this. You are my girl, the only real friend that I've had in a very long time." Her smile slowly faded and her face took on a serious expression. "I remember the day that my husband and my son died. I thought that I was going to be alone in this world because his family can't stand me and I'm not that close with my own family. For months, I was by myself, pregnant and depressed without a soul to talk to about it except Evan. I would sit in the house and rub my belly talking to him but mostly apologizing to him for being such a fuck up. Then that day at the doctor's office God sent you. I am a firm believer that people cross paths in life for a reason and that it's not by mistake. You and I were both going through a rough patch in our lives when we met. He brought us together to help each other through the rough." I saw a tear roll down her cheek and she reached up and wiped it away. Seeing her become emotional cause me to become emotional as well and my eyes started to tear up. Never taking her eyes off of the road, she continued. "The day that I gave birth to Evan, none of Johnathan's family showed their faces and my family showed up late, after everything was over but you were right there by my side from the first labor pain until I pushed him out. I appreciate that more than you could ever know. I say that to say, you have been a good friend to me and been by my side when I've needed you so there is no way in hell that I am not going to be here for you. Now again...if Tre or any of his little ratchet bitches wants to get stupid, we can get stupid right along with them. I ain't saying we gone win the battle but we ain't going out without a bang damn it!"

I burst into laughter and so did she, both of us wiping our tears.

"Nisey, you're a fool!" I shook my head continuing to laugh.

"Yeah, I know." She agreed. "I love you girl."

"I love you too." I looked at my friend and realized that our friendship had become something more. She had become my sister...we were family.

Lala

Nisey woke me up by calling my name just as we turned into Tre's driveway. I sat up, stretched and then glanced at the time on the dashboard clock while rubbing the sleep from my eyes. It was a little after noon. I reached up and flipped down the sun visor and looked in the mirror. I rubbed my hair down because it was a little dishevel and applied some gloss to my lips.

"You good?" Nisey asked running her hands over her hair as well as she looked into the mirror on the driver's side.

"Yeah, I'm good." I replied flipping the sun visor back up. "Thank you so much for driving all the way here. My plan was to let you drive halfway and then take over but obviously I was more tired than I'd thought."

"Girl, it's all good. I didn't mind." She said waving me off and then pointing at the three cars parked in the driveway. "Tre has a lot of company doesn't he?"

"One of those cars belongs to his parents, one belongs to Mina and the cream colored one is his." I told her as I opened up the door to get out. As I stepped out of the car the nervous feeling that I'd been feeling earlier returned. "I sure hope Tre doesn't act stupid and lord knows I hope that his parents haven't allowed him to brainwash them into thinking that I am an unfit mother."

"Girl, don't let that mess worry you, ain't nobody thinking about Tre or his parents. Those are your babies and they need to be back with you. Where was everybody for the first few months of their lives when you were doing everything by yourself? You took damn good care of those girls then and nothing happened to them." She smacked her lips. "Hmph, you are better than me anyways because gun or no gun that nigga wouldn't have taken my babies no damn where."

I saw that she was getting heated and I didn't want her to go inside with an attitude. So I decided to leave the subject alone. As we approached the porch, I heard what sounded like arguing. We walked up on the porch and I was more than sure that was exactly what I was hearing.

"Damn, are they arguing?" Nisey asked her eyes going from me to the door.

"Sounds like it but that ain't got shit to do with me. I came to get my babies and that's what I am going to do." I replied and then rang the doorbell. "They can argue all they want to. That's on them."

"I feel you."

We stood there and waited for someone to answer. After a minute of waiting and listening to them argue back and forth, I rang the bell again. Obviously they couldn't hear for all of the commotion going on in the inside. I heard someone say, "Call their mama if you can't watch them no better than this! They need to be with their mama anyways." The voice sounded like Tre's mama. I rang the bell two more times because it sounded like she was referring to my babies and I wanted to know what in the hell was going on!

"Fuck that bitch! I am capable of taking care of my own damn kids. If she had been watching them instead of leaving them alone with her pussy ass boyfriend then I wouldn't have them!" I heard Tre yell!

"Watch how you come out of your mouth to your mama boy!" That was Mr. Jefferson.

I started to ring the bell repeatedly. I needed to get inside and find out what in the hell was going on with my babies. Apparently something was very wrong judging by how upset everyone on the other side of the door seemed to be. *I knew that I was going to come down here and end up in some bullshit! It never fails!* I thought to myself. This entire situation with Tre was like a never ending soap opera.

"I'm coming gotdamn it! Stop ringing my motherfuckin bell like that?" Tre yelled as he approached the door and then I heard him sliding the chain from the lock. He snatched the door open. "Why in the fuck are you ringing my motherfuckin bell like you've lost your motherfuckin mind?" He roared.

"Because I rung it several times and you didn't hear it." I snapped back at him. I was so over his fucked up attitude! At this point I was willing to go toe to toe with his ass!

"Well if I didn't hear you then you fuckin' stand here and wait until I do but don't be ringing my bell like that!"

Mr. Jefferson walked up behind him. "Hey, Lala."

He spoke. "Tre, you need to calm down. You were already upset before she came. Don't take your anger out on her."

"Hey, Mr. Jefferson." I spoke and then focused my attention back on Tre. "Tre, I didn't come here to argue with you. Where are the girls? I..."

"I don't give a fuck what you came for." He cut me off. "I'm just letting you know..."

"And I'm letting you know too!" I exploded. "I'm sick of your fucked up attitude! Nigga, I fucked up, okay? I made a bad decision but that shit doesn't give you any right to talk to me like I ain't shit because frankly I can remember you making a lot of bad decisions concerning our daughters! So if you feel like I ain't shit because of one mistake then guess what? You ain't shit either!" I told him matter-of-factly. I was sick of him coming at me as if his shit didn't stink. He was on some other shit but it was about time for him to be brought back down to size.

"Bitch..." He charged towards me but didn't have a chance to touch me because Mr. Jefferson grabbed him and pulled him back.

"Boy if you don't get your ass in here and sit down somewhere!" He said pulling Tre back into the house and pushing him up against the wall in the hallway. "I am so sick of your shit! You are twenty-five years old! Act like it because right about now you are acting like a damn child."

"It ain't me it's that bitch!"

"Bitch? She is the mother of your kids! I didn't raise you this way, to be so disrespectful. What kind of example are you setting for your kids by acting the way that you are?" He asked. Tre didn't respond instead he turned his head the other way. "I understand that you are upset by what has happened but this is no way to handle it. As parents when something goes wrong with your children the two of you are supposed to come together and come up with a solution. Not fight each other and one of you snatch the children from the other one. That is not good for them. You are walking around here swollen up with your chest poked out like you are the only one who has been affected by this situation. That woman was the one who laid down and gave birth to those children. So what makes you think that she isn't hurting? You are running around here placing blame and pointing fingers but maybe you should take some time to evaluate your part in all of this."

"My part?" Tre's head snapped around and he looked like he was shocked by what his daddy had just said. "What do you mean my part? They were with her! If they had been with me nothing like that would've ever happened."

"My point exactly!" Mr. Jefferson told him poking him in the chest with his finger. "If you would grow up and stop hopping from bed to bed and woman to woman, maybe you would've been there with her helping her raise your kids instead of another man and this may not have happened."

"So you're saying this is my fault?"

"You're saying that it's her fault, right?"

"It is!" Tre pointed at me spittle, flying from his mouth! I didn't say anything. I just stood there with my arms folded waiting to hear what would come out of his ignorant ass mouth next. "Her stupid ass is the one who left the kids with his pedophile ass! All because she was so desperate for a fucking man!"

"I ain't never been desperate behind no nigga except you triflin' ass and I'm regretting the hell out of that now!"

"Bitch the feeling is mutual!" He shot back. "I should've made you swallow my babies like all of the rest of them, they probably would've been better off!" His last statement left me speechless. I didn't know how to respond because I was too embarrassed.

Mr. Jefferson must've picked up on the look of embarrassment on my face, he shook his head. Just as he opened his mouth to say something, Mrs. Jefferson came down the hallway with Laila in her arms.

"That's enough!" She told Tre. She was holding Laila on her hip. "I've heard enough of this foolishness. The way that you are standing out here disrespecting this girl, doesn't make any sense. What you need to be doing is answering my question about how these bruises got on this here baby's leg!"

"Bruises? What bruises?" I asked rushing over and taking Laila from her arms and examining both of her legs. On her left thigh there were three small bluish black bruises. "What happened to her leg?" I asked looking at Tre and waiting for a reply.

"Yo, for real you can't ask me shit!" He told me and rolled his eyes.

"Oh well, I'm asking you!" I shot back! "Now what happened to my baby's leg?"

"Bitch fuck you!"

"I'll be a bitch and whatever else you want to call me but somebody is going to tell me what happened to Laila's leg."

He chuckled sarcastically. "Yo, you are real funny."

"I don't see anything funny. I am dead serious." I told him shifting my weight from one leg to the other while balancing Laila on my hip. "What happened to her leg?"

He didn't say anything.

"Well, we are waiting? Stop standing there like your mouth is stuck together!" Mrs. Jefferson snapped.

"I told you that Mina said she fell." He answered. "Why are you making such a big deal out of it?"

"I'm not making a big deal out of anything." She corrected him. "I just wanted to know where these bruises came from on my grandbaby."

"How did she fall? Did she land on something when she fell because these bruises are spread out in spots?" I said examining her leg again. This time I noticed another small bruise a little further down her leg from the rest of them.

"I don't know how she fell or what she fell on." He

replied. "Mina said she went to the bathroom and on her way back down the hall she heard her crying. When she got in the living room she was lying beside the sofa crying."

Mrs. Jefferson shook her head. "Something doesn't sound right."

"What do you mean something doesn't sound right?" Tre asked.

"Exactly what I said." She replied. "What I am not understanding is how this baby ended up with not one bruise but several bruises and Mina says she only fell on the floor next to the sofa. Mind you, there is carpet on the floor."

"So again, what are you trying to say?" Tre asked again. "Are you implying that Mina did something to her?"

I was tired of listening to the back and for between Tre and his mama. I decided to go straight to the source. "Excuse me. Let me get past you." I told Mrs. Jefferson.

She stepped back out of the way and I walked past her into the house.

"Hold up. Where in the fuck do you think you are going?" Tre called after me. I ignored him and kept on walking down the hallway towards the living room. "Lala come the fuck up out of my crib!" He continued but I didn't pay what he was saying any mind. When I walked into the living room Mina was sitting on the arm of the sofa, her child-like face held a frightened expression. She rubbed her hands nervously up and the down the pair of faded grey jeans that she was wearing.

"Hey Mina." I spoke stopping directly in front of her.

"Hey Lala." She replied looking everywhere but in my face, which to me was a sign of guilt but I didn't want to jump the gun and accuse her of anything without giving her a chance to explain what had happened. I knew that there was a strong possibility that Laila may have just fallen because it was normal for a child her age to pull up on things and fall but the bruises on her leg didn't look like bruises from a fall. To be honest I couldn't explain what they looked like. What I did know was that normally when someone fell hard enough to bruise themselves it was just one bruise not several small ones. "What happened to Laila's leg?" I asked getting straight to the point.

"I was watching the girls yesterday along with my daughter. They were in here on the floor playing. I had to pee really bad so I left them in here playing while I went to the bathroom." She explained, her eyes roaming back and forth between everyone in the room. Tre, his parents, and Nisey had come inside after me and were listening to her explain as well. "I was on my way back down the hall when I heard Laila start wailing really loudly. I ran in here and saw her lying on the floor. She must've pulled herself up by the sofa and fallen."

"Did you see anything that she may have fallen on?" I asked because that still didn't make any sense to me. That part about her pulling up by the sofa and falling did but the bruises didn't.

"Ummm...uh...ummm...I think there may have been some little wooden blocks that they'd been playing with that she may have fallen on. I assume because she's so light that's why she bruised like that...I guess." I stood there studying her body language. Now she was fidgeting with her hair. I may have been more inclined to believe her story if she wasn't acting so guilty. Something about the shit that she was spitting to me wasn't right but I decided to let it go because I couldn't prove that she was lying.

"Hmph, I see..." I replied shaking my head.

She stood up. "Lala, I swear to you that's what happened. Do you think that I did it or something?" She asked with a wrinkled brow.

"I'm not saying that you did or you didn't but that story doesn't sound right to me." I answered truthfully. "However, I wasn't here and so I can't say what happened."

"I swear on everything, I love that I didn't do nothing to that baby!" She raised her right hand. She looked at Tre. "See this is why I didn't want to be keeping somebody else's kids because of situations like this. Why would I do something to hurt a baby?"

"I didn't say that you did anything to her." I snapped feeling myself become upset because I was trying to let it go and here she was going on and on about it. "I was done with it."

"Yeah but I could tell by your expression and the little remark that you made that you think I did something to her." She accused with tears in her eyes, which didn't make me believe her any more than I did before. My gut was telling me that there was something that she wasn't telling. "I'm not that type of person. I have a child of my own and I would have a fit if someone did something to her. So why would I hurt someone else's baby?"

"Man, don't worry about that bullshit." Tre interjected. He reached over and wiped her tears. "I know that you ain't do shit to Laila. If I thought that you would do something to my kids, I wouldn't have left them here with you."

"You can say whatever you want but I still say she wasn't watching them like she should've been." Mrs. Jefferson said folding her arms. "If she was going to leave the room then she should've put them in the playpen because they could put something in their mouths and swallowed it and choked to death while she was in the bathroom. Luckily it was only a few bruises but it could've been something worse."

"Yeah it could've been worse like having a grown ass man touching on them." Tre said giving me a nasty look.

I'd had enough of all of the drama and going back and forth. That wasn't what I'd come for so I decided to be the bigger person and give the bullshit a rest. It was evident that Tre and I wasn't going to be able to be civilized towards one another anytime soon and I was fine with that. Frankly I didn't give a fuck if he never said anything else to me as long as he was black. I wouldn't try to keep him from his kids but the two of us never had to speak again. "Mina, don't worry about it. Whatever happened, happened. You said she fell while you were in the bathroom, accidents happen." I told her and then turned to Tre. "With that being said. I am done arguing and fussing back and forth. I came here to get my babies and hopefully sit and try to talk with you about how we can co-parent without all of the extra shit."

"Co-parent? You aren't taking my daughters anywhere."

I let out a frustrated sigh. "Tre, I am trying my best to act like an adult here. Can you please try and meet me halfway?" I pleaded with him. "I'm not leaving here without my babies."

"Yeah, you are leaving up out of here and you can

bet your last dollar that you won't be taking Laila and Lola with you."

"Will you please act your damn age instead of your shoe size?" Mr. Jefferson exploded throwing up his hands. "This mess right here isn't making any sense. Those babies need both of their parents, not one. You can't just snatch those kids from their mama boy! What is wrong with you?"

"No disrespect pops but this ain't none of your business." Tre told his dad and walked over to me and attempted to take Laila from my arms but she started squealing and crying. "Come on to daddy Lil' Mama."

"Tre, why don't you stop?" I asked still holding on to Laila, who was holding on to my shirt for dear life. "Tre...please...don't do this. I am not going to leave here without my children. I will call the police or whoever I have to but you will not keep me away from my children."

"Call whoever you need to call. I have just as much

rights to them as you do." He told me and then pulled Laila from my arms. She lost it kicking and throwing a tantrum. "Cut that foolishness out Laila." He raised his voice. "Your mama ain't fit to raise you so you can't go with her."

Without warning Mrs. Jefferson walked up to Tre and slapped the piss out of him. She must've scared Laila because she stop squealing instantly. "Give that baby back to her mama. Right now!" She demanded. "I have never seen anything like this in my life. You are my son and I love you but lord knows all I want to do right now is take your head off of your damn shoulders!"

"Ma..."

"I said give her the damn baby!" She said and hit him again. "I ain't Lala or Kisha! Play with me if you want to and see what happens. They play with your ass but I refuse to. If you want to blame someone for what happened to your daughter blame that sorry no good grown rusty ass man that did it and stop blaming this woman right here!" She pointed to me. "From what her mama told me, when she walked in and caught him touching that child she beat the hell out of him. That doesn't sound like someone who doesn't give a damn or an unfit mama to me. That sounds like a real damn mama to me!"

"It wouldn't have happened if she hadn't left them in the first place!"

"But she did and it did happen!" She didn't back down. "Now are you going to act like a real father and forgive the mother of your children for her mistake or are you going to hold onto it forever and continue to disrespect her in front of your kids forever. Remember they won't be babies forever and pretty soon they will be able to understand the things that you are saying to their mother. Do you want them to hear the disrespectful things that you say to her and start to believe that is how a man is supposed to talk to them? Be careful son because one day your daughters will be women." He didn't say anything he just looked away. "Life doesn't come with a manual baby, we all make mistakes but from those mistakes we learn. If nobody else knows that you should. Let's not forget how Lala ended up as the mother of your children in the first place. Hell, her judgment wasn't perfect when the two of you started messing around so why are you expecting it to be now." I didn't miss the jab that she'd took at me but I couldn't say anything because she had a point. "Go ahead and give her that baby."

Tre walked over and held Laila out for me to take her. I reached out to take her but he didn't let go. Instead he spoke through clenched teeth, staring me directly in my eyes. "Please don't make me have to kill you because if anything else happens to my kids while they are with you, that is exactly what I am going to do. Please take what I am saying to heart because I mean every word." I didn't bother replying, instead I just stood there with my mouth shut and allowed him to say what was on his mind. I figured that way I could avoid another nasty argument and him possibly changing his mind about giving me the girls. "I swear, I regret the day that I ever laid eyes on you and especially the day that I decided to fuck you raw and impregnate you but you best believe this shit right here is a lesson learned because now I have to deal with your triflin' ass for the next eighteen years." He kissed Laila on the cheek. "Daddy loves you, Lil' Mama." He told her and then released the grip that he had on her.

I took her from his arms and then used my hand to swipe away the tears that were rolling down my cheeks. I'd never in my life experienced anyone talking to me the way that he had or hurting me the way that he had but one thing that he'd said was true...this shit was a lesson learned.

Tre went down the hallway and came back with a sleeping Lola in his arms. "Mina, get my keys off of the coffee table and then go outside and get their car seats out of the car." She hurriedly did as he said.

I handed Laila to Nisey and then went outside and got the car seats from Mina and scrapped them in my car. When I was done I put the girls inside. Tre brought their things out to the car while, I waited outside.

When he was finished, he got in his car and left without saying another word. I assumed that he didn't want to be around me another minute and that was fine because I didn't want to be around him either.

"See y'all some other time." I told Mr. and Mrs. Jefferson as I opened my car door to get inside.

"Are you going back to Danville today?" Mrs. Jefferson asked.

"No ma'am, I am staying for a week. I want to spend some time with my parents and allow them to spend a little time with the girls as well before I go back."

"I see." She smiled. "I took the girls by to see your mama the other day when I had them and she and I sat down and had a nice long conversation. She's a really nice lady."

"Yeah she is."

Mrs. Jefferson reached out and pulled me into her arms and hugged me really tight. "I know that the things he said hurt you and I am not trying to make any excuses for him but he only said those things out of anger." She whispered in my ear referring to the things that Tre had said. "I apologize for him."

"It's fine."

She broke our embrace and caressed the side of my face. "You and my grandbabies come and see me before you go back, okay?"

"We will." I promised slipping into the driver's seat. "See you later, Mr. Jefferson."

"See ya, Lala." He replied waving.

I started the car, backed out of the driveway and headed to my parent's house.

Kisha

"Quan if you don't stop that running in this store. I am going to whip your butt right in here in front of all of these people." I warned as I limped faster behind my son and grabbed a hold of his hand to keep him from running off again. I'd left my crutches at home because to be honest I was just plain sick of those things. Plus I hadn't wanted to show up at my interview with them looking handicap. Lord knows I didn't need anything else to make me look bad. It was worse enough that I'd shown up with two kids but I hadn't had any other choice because I didn't have anyone else to watch them. My mama and Tre both had to work. I'd asked Tre's parents but his mama had a doctor's appointment and his daddy had gone with her. So I'd been left with no choice but to bring the boys along.

We were in Walmart. I'd put in an application there a few weeks before and they'd finally called me in for an interview. That morning I'd thought about calling and rescheduling the interview but I needed a job immediately and I didn't have time to be waiting around for another interview. That was if they would've even agreed to reschedule it. Me asking to reschedule may have made it look like I didn't really want the job and I hadn't been willing to take that risk. There were a lot of things that I wanted to do. To begin with, I wanted to be able to take care of me and my kids on my own without having to depend on Tre, my mama or his parents. Secondly, I wanted to get my own place and move out of my mama's crib. I'd began feeling like a bum for being twenty- six years old with two children and living in my mama's crib. I was ready to have my own independence and be on my grown woman shit. It was time for me to get my shit together. Hopefully starting with getting this job at Walmart but I wasn't feeling too good about how the interview had gone. Even though I'd apologized to the hiring manager that interviewed me, for bringing my kids along, her face had still held an agitated expression the entire time. All I could do now though was pray that she would find it in her heart to overlook me bringing my kids to the interview or at least see it as me wanting the job so bad that I didn't let not having a sitter keep me from my interview. I decided to push it to the back of my mind and try not to worry about it. Lord know I already had enough to worry about. The job situation was in God's hands now.

"Ma, I want a game for the Xbox." Shaun announced as he took off and started to run in the direction of the games.

"Shaun get back here!" I called after him. He turned around to look back at me and ran into a woman pushing a stroller. I rolled my eyes up in my head and let out a frustrated breath as I marched towards him and the woman. "I am going to beat his little ass as soon as we get to the damn car." I mumbled under my breath.

"Hey Shaun, are you okay?" The woman was bent down checking to see if he was okay so I couldn't see her face but I was wondering how in the hell she knew my son's name.

"I'm okay." Shaun giggled. "Where is my daddy at? Is he with you?"

"No, I don't know where your daddy is." She

replied.

Just as I reached them, Lala stood up. When she saw me standing directly in front of her the smile that she'd been wearing started to fade.

"Hey Kisha." She spoke.

There was a brown-skinned petite woman with Lala. She spoke as well.

"Hey." I managed to drag out. My nerves were already plucked due to Shaun running off like he was crazy and seeing Lala only plucked my nerves even more. I'd been trying my best to rise above all of the bullshit with her and Tre because I'd finally come to realize that what happened was partially my fault for allowing him to do so much dirt in the past and always taking him back when I knew his ass was up to no good. If it hadn't been her that he'd gotten pregnant it would've eventually been someone else. Still, seeing her infuriated me. Even though I was trying, I knew I wouldn't be able to just put it all behind me overnight and act as if she hadn't fucked my baby daddy knowing that we were together.

"Hey Quan. How have you been Lil' Man?" Lala asked tucking her shoulder length hair behind her ear, the smile that she'd been wearing before returned to her face.

"Fine." He replied shyly hiding behind me and holding onto my shirt.

I turned my attention back to Shaun. I wasn't about to let him off the hook. "Shaun didn't I tell you not to run in this store?" I scolded him.

"Yes ma'am." He gave me his best puppy-dog face. He knew by the look on my face and my tone that he was in trouble.

"Well why were you running then?" He shrugged his shoulders looking up at me with tears in his eyes. "Oh you don't know? That's fine. You will know when I get your tail to that car."

"Girl, you sound just like my mama back in the day." The chic with Lala giggled. "I remember those days all too well. Whenever she would tell me that, I knew that my ass was about to get it when we reached the car."

"Me too." Lala said giggling along with her friend.

I didn't even crack a smile. I just stood there looking back and forth between the two of them. I couldn't bring myself to stand there and be fake like we were cool because we were a long ways from that. I felt like I was doing damn good just by standing there and keeping my hands to myself and my nasty comments in my head. That in itself told me that I'd matured some since the last time that we'd seen each other. "Come on boys." I held out my hand for Shaun to take and he put his and in mine.

"Can I see my sisters?" Quan stepped in front of me and asked Lala just as I was about to turn and walk off.

"Yeah, you sure can. If your mama doesn't mind." She told him and pulled the hood of the stroller back so that he could see them. "Their little fat butts ate and went to sleep." She smiled as she looked at the two sleeping babies with a look of adoration in her eyes. I was glad that Tre had finally come to his senses and allowed her to have them back. Even though I wasn't fond of her, I could tell that she was a good mother and loved her babies.

Quan walked up closer to the stroller and so did Shaun. I felt a pain shoot through my heart as I looked at the girls lying there looking like the perfect mixture of Tre and Lala. They would forever be a constant reminder of Tre's betrayal. The funny thing was that I'd seen these two babies more than a dozen times now but each time that I saw them still hurt just as bad as the first time when I'd seen them in the picture that Lala posted of them on Facebook. I wasn't sure if I'd ever be able to see them and not feel anything. Maybe in time, it wouldn't hurt so badly but I seriously doubted if it would ever completely go away.

I needed to get out of the store and away from Lala and her babies. It was too much. I wasn't strong enough yet to deal with her or them. "Come on boys." I repeated and tugged on their hands.

"Bye Ms. Lala." Shaun told her.

"Bye." Quan waved.

"Bye-bye y'all." She waved at them. "See you later Kisha." I could tell that she was trying to be civilized but it was too much.

"Yeah." I replied and walked off in the other direction without even looking back at her. I was headed in the direction of the exit when I remembered that I needed to grab something to cook for dinner. I turned around and headed back towards the frozen food section. When I got back there I grabbed two packs of chicken and a bag of mixed vegetables and then made my way to the front so that I could checkout.

I was standing in line, flipping through a magazine while waiting to pay for my items when the conversation of the ladies ahead of me grabbed my attention.

"Girl, you are dead wrong." One of the girls

laughed. "You are going to keep right on until somebody whoops your ass."

"Nelle don't try to act all innocent like you have never wanted to snatch a knot in somebody's little bad ass kid." The girl with her replied. Her voice sounded really familiar which caused me to look up. I couldn't see either of their faces because they had their backs to me and there was a man standing between us but I was almost certain that the shortest one was Mina. I rolled my eyes up in my head, and mumbled. "God can't possibly hate me that much to allow me to run into both of these bitches on the same day back to back."

"Yeah, I have wanted to a lot of times. Especially when I am out in a store and somebody's kids are showing their asses, throwing tantrums and shit but that's different. These are two babies that we are talking about. They ain't even one yet. How bad can they be?" Nelle replied to Mina's last comment.

"Shit! They're little asses are bad as hell. Lala done

messed them up. They cry 24/7, girl. I mean, they be crying for nothing at all."

"Mina, you just told me that you be pinching them. That's probably why they be crying."

"I only pinch them when they be crying and won't shut the hell up!" Mina laughed like the shit she was saying was cute. I wanted to beat the brakes off of her no good ass right then and there but I couldn't.

Nelle shook her head while continuing to laugh. "Girl, you'd better be glad they are Lala's kids and not mine because if I was her and I found out you did some shit like that to my babies. I would kill your ass. You seriously need some help. I think being around Mello for all of those years done fucked your head up because you be doing some foul shit and then act as if the shit is cool."

Mina waved her off. "Shit, me pinching them ain't no worse than Lala leaving them with her pedophile ass boyfriend!" The line moved forward and I moved up too being careful to keep the magazine up to my face. I wanted to hear what all her triflin' ass was about to say. I was hoping that she didn't come out of her mouth and admit to doing anything to my children because if she did, she wasn't going to leave out of Walmart walking. Someone was going to be carrying that bitch out of there! Luckily, the boys were busy playing with a little toy that was on the shelf next to the register because it was keeping them quiet. I prayed that her of Nelle wouldn't look back and notice me.

"It doesn't matter now anyways." Mina continued. "She came and got their little crying asses a few days ago. Tre was tripping because he didn't want her to have them but I was like please let her take their asses back with her. I couldn't take all of that damn crying anymore. You should've seen me helping her get their shit!"

"Girl, you have a lot of nerve. I have got to give you that because judging by how upset you say Tre is with Lala, he will probably beat the shit out of you if he finds out that you were pinching and shaking those girls."

Nelle wasn't laughing anymore and her voice held a serious tone to it now. "You had better chill the hell out doing crazy shit."

"Damn Nelle calm down you act like I was beating them or something. I just pinched them a few times and I only shook Laila once." Nelle just shook her head.

This crazy bitch was actually talking like this shit was normal. I'd heard enough! I put the magazine back on the rack and tossed the food that I'd been holding in my arms on the little shelf right next to the counter. I grabbed the boys and started walking towards the door. Right before we reached the exit, I took the toys that they'd been playing with and tossed them on a shelf, never breaking my stride. They started whining, which I'd known they would do, that is why I hadn't taken the toys while we were near Mina and Nelle because I hadn't wanted for either of them to hear the boys and notice me. I had a trick for Mina's ass. I was about to go and let Tre know about all of the shit that she'd been doing to his kids. He'd been running around talking shit about Lala to anyone who would listen and had been ready to beat my ass for trying to get him to get him to see that anybody could make the mistake of misjudging someone. I wondered what he was going to say when he found out that he'd been sleeping with the enemy all along.

When I reached my car, I unlocked the doors and rushed the boys inside. "Get in and buckle your seatbelts." I told them as I held the door for them to get into the backseat. Once they were inside, I closed the door and opened my door to get in.

"Excuse me...excuse me beautiful." A deep baritone voice called from behind me.

I turned to see if the person was referring to me. When I turned around there was this tall brown skinned brother with almond shaped brown eyes staring back at me. The goat-tee that he sported on his face was trimmed to perfection. It looked like he'd just stepped out of the barber's chair. He wore a black NY fitted on his head pulled down low to the point that I just could see his eyes.

"Are you talking to me?" I asked hoping to God that he was because the brother was fine as hell. He kind of put me in the mind of a young Morris Chestnut.

"Yes, I most certainly was." He replied flashing a smile which also revealed a set of adorable dimples.

Damn this motherfucka is fine as hell. I thought to myself. *If fine was a crime, his sexy ass would be doing life!* He was so fine that I'd momentarily forgotten all about Mina's triflin' ass and the things that she'd just bragged about doing to the girls.

"I couldn't help but notice you on my way inside the store. You are so fine that I had to turn around and introduce myself." He continued to smile and extended his hand for me to shake. "My name is Lavar."

"Hey Lavar, I'm Kisha." I reached out and shook his hand. When my hand touched his a chill ran down my spine.

"It's very nice to meet you, Ms. Kisha. Do you have a significant other or someone special in your life at the moment?"

"No, I don't actually." I blushed.

"Hmmm...I see." He licked his full lips. "How old are you?"

"I'm twenty-six and you?"

"I'm thirty-one." He replied. "Is that too old for you?"

"No, not at all."

"Okay, well do you a number where I could call you and get to know you better?" He asked. "It's kind of cold out here so I won't hold you long. I wouldn't want you to catch a cold. At least not until you trust me enough to take care of you and nurse you back to good health." I blushed harder. I was kind of feeling him and even though at this point I was trying to concentrate on getting my life on track for me and my boys. It couldn't hurt to go out and get to know him. I told him my number and he programmed it in his phone. "Okay then beautiful. I will give you a call later." He told me as he slipped his phone back in his pocket.

"Okay cool, I will talk to you later then."

"Alright drive safely and enjoy the rest of your day." He told me and then walked off in the direction of the store. I got in my car and headed to Tre's house.

Mina

"Nelle it's really not that big of a deal." I told her as we walked across Walmart's parking lot towards her car. The wind was blowing a little and the chilly breeze cut

185

right through the thin top that I was wearing. I'd left my jacket in my car which was at Tre's house. I walked a little faster trying to hurry and get to the car. "I think you are over-reacting just a little. I didn't abuse their little asses. I just simply let them know that I am not their mama and I refuse to put up with all of that unnecessary crying and whining."

Nelle hit the button on the remote on her keychain to unlock the doors and then opened the trunk. We both started taking the stuff out of the basket and placing it in the trunk. "Mina, I'm not over-reacting because really it isn't any of my business. All I am saying is that if you feel like they cry too much or that you don't like watching them, then why not just tell Tre that instead of pinching them or shaking them. What if something happens to them while they are in your care? Do you know what could happen to them as a result of you shaking them? That could cause brain damage or even kill them." She briefly glanced back at me over her shoulder.

I smacked my lips and rolled my eyes before bursting into laughter. She was standing here in front of me sounding like a fucking after school special. "Lawd girl, you have been watching way too much TV. I didn't shake them that damn hard. I only shook them to scare them a little and make them shut the hell up." I told her uptight ass. If you asked me, she needed to shake or pinch Korey's little spoiled ass because her and Corey had messed that child up too. Every time I went over to their house or they brought her little ass over to mines, I ended up with a migraine due to her crying and whining every second about something that they wouldn't let her spoiled ass have or do.

Nelle let out a sigh and threw up her hands before closing the trunk. "Okay Mina but don't say that I didn't try and warn you. You know what they say, a hard head makes a soft ass. You gone learn to listen one day. I have no idea where you got that damn stubbornness from but suit yourself. I just hope that Tre doesn't catch you pinching or shaking them because if he does he is going to kill your ass." She cut her eyes at me as she walked around and got in on the driver's side.

I rolled my eyes up in my head, pushed the basket out of the way and then got in on the passenger side. "Girl, I ain't thinking about Tre. He shouldn't have went and snatched them from their mama and then expected for everybody else to help him keep them." I buckled my seatbelt. "Shit, I ain't nobody's damn live in babysitter. I don't be dropping Simya off on him!"

She was backing out but then brought the car to a halt. "So you are going to sit here and lie like Tre don't be watching Simya for you?"

"I don't ask him though." I let her know.

"Exactly, he does it and you don't even have to ask. Mind you, she isn't his so that isn't his responsibility." She swiveled her neck like she was checking me or something. "That man helps you take care of your child financially and he takes her places with him and his kids.

He doesn't have to do that." She paused and shook her head. "I don't know what Mello did to you but you had better get your shit together before you end up making someone fuck you up. I don't know why you do the stuff you do. I hope and pray that you never do any crazy shit to me because if you ever cross me in some fucked up way I am going to beat the dog shit out of you. Point blank period." She told me matter-of-factly.

I studied her face and saw that she meant business. I started to become a little bit nervous. I really wasn't sure of how of how I should respond to that. "Damn, it's like that? You are getting upset with me and threatening me for pinching those kids? You act like, I abused them. It really wasn't that serious."

"I am not upset with you nor am I threatening you. I am just letting you know." She corrected me. "You are my cousin and I love you to death but you be doing way too much. It's obvious that man trusts you because he is leaving you alone with his kids. After everything that has happened with Lala and the whole situation with her boyfriend touching one of them, why would you even do something like that? Maybe you didn't pinch them hard or shake them too roughly but the point is that you did it at all. You wouldn't want anyone pinching or shaking Simya. All I'm saying is you need to chill out before you fuck with the wrong person."

I didn't bother to say anything. I just turned my head and looked out the window. For the first few minutes of the drive, neither of us said anything else. I was looking out the window and wishing that she'd hurry up and get me to my destination so that I could get from around her uppity ass. If I'd know that she was going to react the way that she had, I would've never told her about what I'd done. I'd thought that she was going to just laugh it off because to me the shit was funny but I should've known that her righteous ass wouldn't. That was the one thing that I hated about her, how she always tried to act like she was perfect and like her shit didn't stink. You would think that she'd never done anything that wasn't right. I knew better than that though, she had the nerve to try and judge me after all of the crazy shit that she done to try and get Corey. Her silly ass had even taken a damn overdose to try and get his attention but I guess she'd forgotten all about her bullshit being that he'd finally felt sorry enough for her thirsty ass to marry her. I couldn't stand folks like her who tried to act like they were better than the next motherfucka knowing that they truly wasn't.

"I hope you aren't mad Mina but I am just keeping it real with you." She spoke. "I'm not trying to talk down to you or anything like that. We all got a little bit of shit with us and we all do foul shit but you went a little bit too far this time cuz, I'm just saying."

Why can't you just shut the fuck up and let the shit go. You've made your fuckin' point! I thought to myself still looking out the window. "I'm not mad." I lied. "I feel what you are saying."

"Really or are you just saying that?"

I turned to look at her. "Yeah, I get it. Maybe I shouldn't have pinched them but at the time they deserved it." I giggled to try and kill the tension between us and at the same time make her think that I wasn't mad. I figured why be mad when I could get even. I'd made it up in my mind that I was going to have the last laugh in the end because I was so sick of her always judging everybody else because she and Corey had finally gotten their fucked up relationship in order. If I had to drug Corey and fuck him. I was going to do it and then take pictures of him naked in my bed and send them to her. A smile formed on my lips as I imagined the look on her face when she saw those pictures. I had news for her perfect ass and I would gladly take the ass whooping that I knew was sure to follow. It would be worth it just to see her perfect little world come crumbling down around her.

"What? What are you smiling about?" She asked

looking at me skeptically.

"Nothing. I am just glad that you and I are able to have a disagreement, work through it and move on. Ya know?" I looked at her my head slightly cocked to the side and a smile plastered on my face.

"Yeah but that's how it should be. We are family. We shouldn't let little things come between us. And we should always be able to be truthful with each other." Her cell phone rang interrupting her little "we are family" speech. She picked it up from her lap, where it had been lying and answered it. "Hello...oh hey Mia." I rolled my eyes and looked back out the window. Mia still wasn't fucking with me like that and frankly I didn't give a fuck. She was just like Nelle always pretending to be perfect. For the most part she had always been a 'good girl' but still that gave her no right to try and look down on me. She was still all in her feelings about the whole Corey situation. As far as I was concerned she could stay in them. What I did with Corey wasn't any of her damn business. If Ron was more of my type I would've tried to give him a shot of pussy too just because of her little stank ass attitude. If she kept it up I might just do it anyways. She and Nelle killed me with all that "we are family" bullshit. Family crossed family every day in the real world. The two of them were just living in a fuckin fantasy world. I'd been stopped giving a fuck about family years ago after sitting around listening to them talk about me and call me names because of my decision to stay with Mello and try to have a family. On numerous occasion, several family events, they would all sit around and talk about me as if I wasn't there. Even though Nelle and Mia would always come to my rescue whenever Mello would beat my ass, the two of them would talk about me right along with everybody else. It'd always been amazing to me how people never took time to think of how much their words could hurt a person. A lot of the things that I'd overheard them saying still stuck with me to that day and they still hurt whenever I thought about it. That was part of the reason why I didn't give a flying fuck about anyone else or their feelings because no one had ever really 100% given a fuck about me. Either they would say they did and their actions said something different or they would pretend to through their actions but something different would come out of their mouths.

"Mina and I are on our way back from Walmart. She had to pick up a few things and I picked up a few cases of soda for the little get together that I am having for my birthday. What are you doing?" Nelle told Mia and then she was was silent for a few seconds while she listened to whatever Mia was saying on the other end. "Do you think you and Ron would feel up to coming by later and playing cards with Corey and me? We haven't gotten together in quite a while. Maybe Tre and Mina could come too." My head snapped around and she looked over at me showing all thirty-two. "We could have a few drinks and just chill." She paused again. "Alright then, it's a date. See y'all a little bit later on." She disconnected the call just as we were turning in Tre's driveway. She parked beside my car and turned off the ignition. "So do you think, you and Tre might want to come over later and play cards with us?"

"Yeah, I guess so." I picked up my pocketbook off the floor of the car and took out the blunt that I'd rolled earlier. I held it up. "You want to smoke?"

"Hell yeah, I want to smoke. Put some fire to that shit." She replied moving the seat back some and adjusting it to get comfortable. Then she reached over and turned the radio on. K. Michelle's joint V. S.O.P was on.

"Oh snap turn that shit up!" I demanded as I put some fire to the end of the blunt and took a few puffs. She did as I asked. "That's my shit right there!" I passed her the blunt and began to dance in my seat while singing along to the song and snapping my fingers. She danced and sang too. We sat there listening to the radio dancing and singing before long the blunt was gone and we both sat in the car high as a kite.

"Damn girl, that shit got my face feeling numb." Nelle admitted giggling and rubbing her face.

I giggled too. "That's because you are used to smoking that bullshit with Corey." I teased. "That right there we just smoked is that good shit. Tre gets it from some dude over in North Carolina."

"Oh for real? I'm going to have to holla at Tre. I need some of that in my life." She continued to rub her hands down her face.

"Are you okay?"

"Yeah, I'm straight." The weed had me feeling really relaxed and my lips started to get loose like they always did whenever I smoked or drank. I leaned back in my seat and looked over at Nelle debating whether or not I should tell her what I'd been wanting to tell her for the past few days. I didn't feel like hearing another speech but I needed to tell someone. "Can I tell you something without you judging me?" I blurted.

"Oh lord…" She rolled her eyes up in her head and threw up her hands dramatically. "Heffa what have you done now?"

The weed had me extra goofy so I just laughed at her dramatic ass. "I haven't done anything." I replied honestly because really I hadn't.

"You've done something." She contested pointing an accusing finger at me. "I know your ass like the back of my hand and I can tell by the way that you started off, you've done something. Talking about me not judging you."

"Well you do always judge me."

She waved me off. "That's all in your head. You are just a very defensive person." She said. "Now tell me the business."

"I've been talking to someone for the past few days on Facebook."

"Someone like who?" She inquired looking at me through low chinky eyes. I could tell she was feeling really good. "Mina, Tre is going to fuck you up!"

"See? This is why I hate telling your dramatic righteous ass anything!" I told her smacking my lips. "Damn you haven't even heard who it is yet and already you are judging me."

"Bitch, I ain't judging you! I am warning you!" She giggled. "It doesn't matter who this nigga is. You know Tre ain't gone be feeling you talking to the next nigga. I mean that's just common sense, it doesn't have anything to do with me being righteous. And stop saying that bullshit too. You've said that shit quite a few times over the past few weeks that I am righteous and think I never do anything wrong. That couldn't be further from the truth. I don't think I am better than anyone and yes I make mistakes but there is a difference between making mistakes and just doing dumb shit! You my dear just be doing dumb shit!"

"What?" I felt some type of way by her last statement. Just because I chose to do what made me happy didn't mean the things I did were dumb.

"You heard me, you be doing dumb shit!" She repeated but it wasn't in a harsh tone. Actually she had a smile on her lips. "Now who is it?"

"Nevermind..." I wasn't about to tell her who it was so she could go on and on about how I as so wrong for talking to him. "Can you pop the trunk so I can get my stuff, please?"

"Oh so now you aren't going to tell me?"

"Nah because I don't feel like another speech or having you blow my high."

"Lord have mercy! Girl, are you seriously upset because I said Tre is going to be mad if he finds out that you are talking to someone else? Do you think that he is going to be happy?"

"Nah but don't you think I already know all of that?" I snapped opening the car door to get out but then paused. "You know, I don't fuck with a lot of people. Only you and Mia...well mainly you, so that is why I come to you and tell you everything because truthfully I don't have anyone else to tell shit to. If I told Mia, of course she would have her nose turned up and looking at me sideways. She has always been the judgmental type but you weren't. Back in the day you were just like me. You did dumb shit and made stupid decisions but now that things are all good in your world you have forgotten all about that. You used to tell me a lot of shit and I never judged you, even when I felt like the shit was stupid. I would listen and give you the best advice I could and then let you do you. Sometimes, I want you to just listen and then allow me to do me. Realize that you and I are different so what may work for you don't necessarily work for me."

"Are you done?"

"Yeah..." I rolled my eyes feeling a lot better after getting some of the stuff off of my chest that I'd been wanting to say for quite some time. I'd wanted to say more but was afraid that if I did things might end up getting physical.

"First of all, I am going to tell you again that I am not judging you. To keep it one hundred with you, you are grown as hell so regardless of what I say you are going to do whatever it is that you want. When you tell me the dumb shit that you be doing or thinking of doing I only try and warn you that you are making a mistake because like you said back in the day I did a lot of dumb shit. So I have been there and done majority of the dumb shit that you are doing. However if you feel like I am always judging you to the point where we have to go through this right here...keep your business to yourself and all of this can be avoided."

"Fine."

"Cool." She got out of the car and opened the trunk for me. Instead of helping me get my stuff she got back in the car and waited until I got my stuff. When I was done she backed out of the driveway without saying another word.

"Stupid bitch." I mumbled as I sat my stuff down on the porch and fumbled around in my pocketbook to find my key. I found it and unlocked the door. Just as I was about to step inside the house, I heard a car pull into the driveway. I turned around with my hands full of bags to see Kisha getting out of her car. "Uggh...what does this hoe want?"

"Is Tre here?" She snapped not bothering to speak with her rude ignorant ass.

I ignored her rudeness because it was evident that she was not going to get over the fact that I was fuckin her babydaddy any time soon. I almost wanted to burst into laughter because she was all upset over some shit that she couldn't do shit about. "No he's..." She turned and limped off not giving me a chance to finish my sentence. "Well fuck you too."

She stopped and looked back. "Did you say something?" I just shook my head. "Oh okay, that's what I thought."

I went ahead in the house. I didn't have time for Kisha's ignorance. She was always running around like she was the baddest bitch in Boykins. I couldn't wait for somebody to beat her ass. I slammed the bags that I had in my hands down on the sofa. I'd had enough of everybody for one day. My phone dinged letting me know that I had a notification. I checked it and saw that it was a messaged from my Facebook messenger. I opened it up...it was from Parnell. A smile spread on my lips.

The message read: *What's up ma? How is your day going? You know I can't wait to see your fine ass when I come home in three weeks. We're still on right?"*

I flopped down on the sofa and messaged him back.

Tre

I sat at Ms. Lizzy's table across from Tyson sipping on a double shot of gin. He was doing the same. I'd gotten off from work early because I had a lot on my mind and it had been hard to stay focus all day. For some reason, I was missing Casper a lot these days. I missed being able to go to him and talk about all of the bullshit that I had going on in my life. He'd always been there to help me sort through my problems and come up with a solution. Whether or not I took his advice had always been on me but he'd always been there to give it. I wished that I could turn back the hands of time and undo a lot of the shit that I'd done. I definitely wouldn't have fucked Tamika! I would've let her go ahead and tell Kisha about Lala. The way I looked at is was, Kisha ended up finding out anyways, I'd still ended up losing my family, along with my best friend and she'd ended up losing her life. The only thing that we'd managed to do was make a bad situation worst. When I thought about it, I felt like coward ass nigga for even allowing Tamika to blackmail me in the first place. I should've handled the entire situation differently than what I had. I shook my head picking up my drink, I down the rest of it. I'd been consistently making fucked up decisions for the past two years, even when I thought I was making the right decisions, I'd been making the wrong ones.

"Hey Ms. Lizzy, can I get another double shot of gin please." I asked. She was seated on one of the barstools next to the island that sat in the kitchen watching a small old fashioned TV, wearing a colorful scarf around her hair. A long silver braid hung from beneath the scarf and rested on her shoulder. I watched as she slid down off of the stool still staring back at the fuzzy picture on the TV screen.

"I love me some George Jefferson." She laughed revealing a mouthful of snuff as she came over and took my cup. "You are doing an awful lot of drinking today Tre. What seems to be the problem? Is one of them gals that you got them babies by worrying you?" She pried walking over to the cabinet, taking down the half gallon of gin and pouring my drink. She put the top back on, placed the bottle back in the cabinet, brought my drink back over to me and placed it in front of me on the table.

"Thank you." I told her before raising my cup and taking a sip of my drink. I decided to answer the question that she'd asked me. "Ms. Lizzy everything seems to be the problem these days."

She walked over to the trashcan and spit a mouthful of snuff juice into it. I remembered being disgusted by her snuff dipping in the past but over the years I gotten used to it and it didn't even faze me anymore. "Is that so?" She stood next to the island with her hand on her hip studying me. She'd always reminded me of the mama from Soul Food except she was a little bit heavier than her.

"Yes ma'am." I nodded and then hung my head and allowed it to rest on my hands. I truly felt as if the weight of the world was on my shoulders.

"Tre, man maybe you've had enough to drink." Tyson suggested.

"I'm good man." I replied lifting my head and

reaching for my drink. I took another sip. My phone rang, I took it from the clip and looked at the name that was flashing on the screen. It was Kisha. I didn't feel like dealing with her. I had too much on my mind already and knowing her she would only add to it. The two of us hadn't talked since the little altercation at my place the previous week and I still didn't have anything to say to her. I needed a break from her and Lala for a little while. I needed time to clear my head before I flipped out and killed someone. I put my phone back in its clip. "Shit just seems to get harder and harder. I can't catch a break for shit."

"You know son, sometimes life is so hard because we make it that way." Ms. Lizzy said taking a seat at the table with Tyson and me. "I bet most of the problems that you have, you brought them on yourself. As a matter of fact, I know for a fact that you did. Ms. Lizzy might be old but I keep these here ears to the streets." She tapped a finger on her ear. "There ain't too much that goes on that I don't know about."

"Can't believe everything that you hear." I told her.

"Nah, you're right but hell everybody in town done seen you bouncing from woman to woman for the past few years and in just the past few months you've switched up two or three times. After a while all of that bouncing around starts to catch up to you and cause a lot of friction. Baby, it ain't what you do, it's how you do it. You have been doing a lot and going about all of it all wrong. Opening up multiple doors before closing one. You can't run around playing with people's feelings and betraying people and think that all of that ain't gone come back to bite you." She paused for a minute and just looked off into space. Her face held an expression that was unreadable and that made me feel a little uneasy. Finally she looked back at me. "Not too long ago you and Skeet got into it right here at this card table over that gal that you got them babies by." She shook her head. "I stood back and watched as everyone rushed to break it up and thought to myself that the both of you were pure sad and should be ashamed. Here y'all were fighting and carrying on like two complete strangers when you've known each other your whole entire life. All I kept praying was that it didn't end like things had between you and Casper."

"He started it! He disrespected my babymama!" I interrupted raising my voice. She touched a nerve with the comment about Casper.

"You disrespected her first." She countered looking me directly in my eyes speaking calmly. "You disrespected her numerous times for everyone to see. You've slept with damn near every little slut in Boykins, including your best friend's woman. To top it all off, you went out and got another woman pregnant and if that wasn't enough you moved the woman in the home that you once shared with her." She let out a little chuckle. "Y'all youngins kill me preaching about respect when you don't know the first thing about it! Now you are sitting

210

here talking about how hard your life is. Baby, you ain't seen hard yet. You gone see all the wrong that you've done to others. Remember you get back what you put out. I ain't trying to be mean nor am I sitting here judging you because I am not in a position to judge anyone but I believe in calling things like I see it. You had to know that one day karma was going to come back around and pay you a visit."

I was about to respond but was distracted by the ringing of my phone. I took it out of the clip and saw Kisha's name flashing across the screen again. My gut told me that something had to be wrong for her to keep calling me and the first thing that came to mind was my boys. I pressed send to answer the call and put the phone up to my ear as I rose from my seat and headed towards the door so that I could talk in private.

"Hello." I spoke into the phone.

"Hey, I need to talk to you about something important concerning your kids." She said with a hint of urgency in her voice.

"So...talk. Are they alright?"

"I'm not talking about Quan and Shaun." She replied causing me to become confused. "I'm talking about the girls."

"Huh? The girls?" I questioned. "What about them? Stop stalling and tell me what the deal is."

"Well, I was in Walmart today and I saw Mina and Nelle. I was behind them in the checkout line but they didn't see me." She explained. "Anyways, I was standing there and overheard Mina bragging to Nelle about how she'd shaken the girls and pinched them while they were at your house. I assume you left them with her."

"Hold the fuck up? What did you just say? Kisha don't play like that!" I snapped. I'd been feeling a little tipsy when I'd first answered the phone but hearing this had somehow managed to sober me up. The day that Lala had come to pick up the girls popped into my head. I couldn't help but think about how suspicious my mom had been of Mina's story about Laila falling and how Lala had questioned it as well. Now hearing Kisha say that she'd heard Mina bragging about pinching the girls and shaking them made me wonder if that is what had caused the bruises that were on Laila's leg. The anger that was building inside of me was so great that it scared me because I wasn't sure if I'd be able to control myself if what Kisha was telling me turned out to be true. I needed to be sure that Kisha was telling the truth. For Mina's sake I prayed that she wasn't. "How do you know she was talking about my girls?"

"Tre, I am not playing! I heard this shit with my own two ears. That's my good word! This ain't no he-say, she-say. I know she was talking about your girls because she said that the reason she was pinching and shaking them was because they wouldn't stop crying all the time. She said Lala had messed them up, I guess meaning she'd spoiled them." She swore and I could tell she was serious. "As a matter of fact, I will tell it in her damn face! You are acting like you don't believe me or something! I don't have shit to lie about. I am telling you because I think that it's fucked up and also to warn you that if she puts her hands on my kids somebody is going to be walking slow behind that bitch and you too. Real talk! Now you can either handle that bitch or I will. I started to fuck her up earlier but I wanted to let you deal with it being that you brought this bitch into the picture and you were the one who trusted her with your kids. Plus, I tried to warn you about that no good bitch the other week but you wasn't trying to hear shit that I was saying. I knew her ass couldn't be trusted. Anybody who will fuck..."

"Kisha will you please shut the fuck up!" I cut her off! That shit that she was going on and on about was irrelevant at the moment. Right now all I was concerned about was confronting Mina about the things that she'd supposedly overheard her bragging about earlier. All of the other shit could wait. "I'm on my way to the crib right now. She is supposed to be there."

"Yeah she's there." She assured me.

"How do you know?"

"Because I went by there looking for you before I called."

Hearing that she'd gone to my house left no questions in my mind about whether or not she'd heard Mina say some foul shit but still I wanted to give Mina a chance to explain...before I fucked her up! "Okay well like I said, I'm on my way to the crib now. You meet me there and we gone get to the bottom of this shit." I didn't wait for her to respond. I disconnected the call and went back into the house. "Yo Tyson come on man, I need to roll out. I got some shit that I need to take care of back at the crib."

He stood to his feet and downed the rest of his drink. "Is everything alright man? Is something wrong with one of the kids?"

"Nah, everything straight." I didn't want to talk about my business in front of Ms. Lizzy, it was obvious that she already knew too much as it was. I reached in my pocket and took out a twenty dollar bill and handed it to Ms. Lizzy for me and Tyson's drinks. "Here you go Ms. Lizzy. You can keep the change."

I started towards the door with Tyson right behind me. "Are you sure that everything is alright?" Ms. Lizzy called behind us.

"Yeah." I replied but never stopped walking. I was getting in the car and heard Ms. Lizzy call my name. I looked up to see her standing on the porch her floral housecoat swaying in the breeze.

"Tre, don't forget what I said to you. The choices that you make are what makes your life so hard. I don't know what that phone call was about but I can tell that whatever it was, it wasn't good. Before you do anything stupid think about whether or not you want to make things harder than what they are. Sometimes the best decision we can make is to walk away from it all."

"Alright...I hear you."

"Don't just hear me, Tre. Listen to what I am saying and take it in."

"Okay." I didn't wait for her to say anything else. I got in the car and left.

A few miles up the street, Tyson asked. "What's going on?"

"Nothing man." I didn't want to drag him into anymore of my bullshit than I already had. "I am going to drop you off at your house."

"Man, cut the bullshit and tell me what's going on. Who was that that called you?" He looked over at me, his dark eyes locked on me waiting for a response.

"Tyson..."

"Nigga what the fuck is going on?" He roared. "Why you acting all secretive and shit?"

I let out a frustrated breath. "I just don't want to drag you into anymore of my shit. I don't want to drag anybody into anymore of my shit."

"Nigga just tell me what the fuck is going on? I am a

grown ass man. You can't drag me into shit that I don't want to be a part of. You don't make any decisions for me, I do." He told me not letting up. "Now do you have some beef with some niggas or something? If so we can handle that shit."

"Nah it ain't nothing like that." I began. "Kisha called and told me that earlier today she was in the store and overheard Mina bragging to her cousin about how she'd shaken and pinched the girls while I had her watching them."

His eyes nearly bulged out of their sockets. "Man say word!"

"That's my word." I nodded my head as I made a left onto his street.

"Where are you going?"

"To take you home."

"Nah umma ride with you to make sure that you don't end up in jail."

"I am going to give her the opportunity to explain

this shit." I made a right at the end of the street and drove in the direction of my house. "The fucked up thing is, I can't for the life of me understand why she would do some fucked up shit like that. She knows the shit that I just went through with Lala about my kids. Not only that but I treat her fuckin' kid like she's my own. What would make her do some foul shit like that to mine?"

Tyson shook his head. "Man, I have no idea why people do the shit that they do." He looked out the window and then back at me. "You are talking like you are already sure that she did it without even hearing her side of things. How do you know that Kisha ain't lying? You know she feels some type of way about you being with Mina in the first place. She could be making this whole story up to come between y'all because she knows how you are when it comes to your kids."

He had a good point and I would've thought the same thing if it hadn't been for the bruises that were on Laila's leg. "I feel what you are saying but the reason why

I believe Kisha is because number one she said that she'd tell the shit in Mina's face."

"But Mina is terrified of Kisha, so that doesn't count. Of course she will tell it to her face. What is Mina going to do about it even if she is lying?" He interjected.

"That's true." I agreed nodding my head. "Well I also believe her because last week my mama had kept the girls for a little while on Saturday morning, when she brought them back she brought to my attention some bruises that she'd noticed on Laila's leg. Well Mina had already mentioned something about Laila falling the day before when she was watching them so I didn't think much of it but my mama wasn't feeling her story. She kept saying that it didn't sound right because the bruises were like three little small circles right together then there was another little one a little bit further down. When Lala arrived she looked at the bruises and said the same thing as my mama. That it didn't look like bruises from a fall. Mina swore up and down that Laila had fallen.

After hearing Kisha's story about Mina pinching the girls, it sounds to me that may have been where the bruises came from."

"Damn..." Tyson replied when I was done. "Yeah that does sound like it could very well be what happened but don't go in here and immediately flip out on her. Give her the chance to explain and pay close attention to both of their body language. You can normally tell when someone is lying because they will be extra nervous, stammering over their words and fidgeting."

"I'm not going to go in and flip. Like I said I am going to give her a chance to tell her side."

We'd arrived at my house by now. I turned in the driveway and parked next to Kisha's car. She was sitting inside waiting. I didn't see the boys in the car with her so I assumed that they were with her mama.

I opened the car door to get out but Tyson reached over and grabbed my arm. "Tre even if you find out that she did do the shit, don't lose your cool. Just tell her to get her shit and get the fuck out. Don't put your hands on her because if you do your ass is going to be right in jail with her babydaddy. You already know this bitch loves to call the police."

I knew that he was right but I wasn't sure if I could promise him that I wouldn't flip out and whoop her ass. "I'll try." I decided to keep it one hundred with him.

"Don't try. Keep your hands to yourself." He said as we both got out of the car. "I know you don't want to hear this but Ms. Lizzy was right. You are the only one who can determine whether shit gets better or worse for you. If you find out she did it, let the bitch go and keep it moving. Don't make shit worse." He warned.

I didn't respond. I just headed towards the house.

Tre

I used my key to let myself in. Kisha and Tyson

followed me inside. "Y'all can have a seat. I'll be right

back. I'm going to get Mina."

"Tre, that bitch better not come out here and try to lie. I'm not playing." Kisha warned. "I know what I heard."

"Calm down and have a seat." I told her. "I didn't call you here to fight. I called you here because I want to know the truth and find out what type of person I've been having round my kids. So no matter what I need you to try and keep your temper under control."

She smacked her lips, folding her arms over her chest. "I'm going to try but I can't promise you anything."

"Alright."

They both took a seat on the sofa and I went down the hall to the bedroom. I pushed the door opened and found Mina stretched out across the bed in her bra and panties messing with her phone. "Put some clothes on and come in the living room. I need to holla at you about something." I told her.

"Why can't you holla at me in here?" She asked

never taking her eyes off the phone. She giggled at something on her phone. "I don't feel like getting up or putting any clothes on. And why do I need to put clothes on anyways."

"Because Tyson is in the living room." I didn't mention Kisha on purpose.

"Tyson?" She finally looked up wearing a confused expression but still didn't bother to move. "What could you possibly want to holla at me about in front of Tyson?"

"Mina stop asking so many damn questions and put some clothes on." I snapped. "I'm not in the mood."

She tossed the phone onto the bed and sat up. "Uh-uhhh don't come up in here with no fuckin' attitude with me for no damn reason because I haven't done shit to you. I was laying in here minding my own fuckin' business. Now I don't know who done pissed you off or got on your bad side but whoever it was you need to go right back out in the streets and take that shit up with them!"

I momentarily visualized myself wrapping my hands around her little neck and choking the life out of her but I managed to remain calm. "Mina get dressed and come in the living room or don't get dressed, it doesn't matter but I am going to holla at you about what I need to holla at you about in the next few minutes whether you are dressed or not."

"Ugggh..." She huffed and jumped up off the bed grabbing her pants off the chair and slipping them on. "What in the fuck is so gotdamn important that you can't just say that shit in here? Why we got to be in front of Tyson? I don't even know that nigga like that so I can't begin to think of what the fuck could possibly be going on concerning him and me both!" She continued to bitch while getting dressed. Little did she know the whole reason for having Tyson present was for her benefit, to keep me from losing it and stomping a hole in her ass if she confirmed that what Kisha was saying was true.

"I'll be in the living room." I told her.

"Whatever…" She pulled her shirt on over her head.

I walked out of the room leaving the door opened and went back into the living room. Kisha and Tyson were both sitting on the long sofa, neither of them saying a word. It was getting dark so I walked over and turned on the lamp that sat in the corner and then took a seat in the recliner that sat across from the sofa.

About a minute passed before I heard Mina stomping down the hallway mumbling. She walked into the living. "What is so damn import…" Her eyes landed on Kisha. "Um-um…what's going on?" She looked around nervously still standing in the doorway. I could tell that all sorts of things were racing through her mind trying to figure out why Kisha was there.

"Come on in and have a seat." I told her. This time she didn't get slick at the mouth she just did as she was told and took a seat on the loveseat. "In the room, I told you that I needed to holla at you about something. Well Kisha called me a little while ago and told me something that she overheard earlier and I am praying to God that she heard wrong because if not, you and me are going to have a serious problem."

"Well Tre, you know how folks lie around here in Boykins..."

"Bitch shut up!" Kisha cut her off slipping to the edge of the sofa. "This ain't nothing that somebody told me! This is something that I heard come directly out of your mouth." Mina looked at me nervously still wearing a confused expression. "Don't look stupid now. You weren't looking stupid earlier today when you were up in Walmart bragging to your cousin about how you pinched and shook Laila and Lola!" Mina's mouth dropped opened. She looked at me like she wanted to speak, her mouth even moved but nothing came out. "I dare you to sit here and say that you didn't say it! I will bust you right in yo' damn mouth! I was standing right behind the two of y'all in the checkout line. Y'all were so busy laughing about the fucked up shit that you'd done to those babies that you didn't even take notice of your surroundings. If you had you would've seen me."

I sat there watching Mina, waiting for her to at least deny it. Even though Kisha had threatened her if the shit wasn't true then she still should've said it but she didn't. Instead tears fell from her eyes and her lips trembled.

"Well Mina is it true? Did you really do some fucked up shit like that to my kids?" I asked looking over at her chewing on my bottom lips. With each second that passed I could feel my anger building.

"Tre...I-I...it ain't like you think. I was only...I didn't pinch them hard. I just..." She didn't get the rest of the sentence out of her mouth before I dived over on the loveseat where she was and slapped her ass so hard that she flipped over the back. I jumped right over the back and snatched her up by her hair and slapped the shit out of her again.

"You raggedy bitch! I trusted your no good ass around my kids and this is what you do?" I slapped her again! She put her hands up and tried to shield her face from the blows.

"Stop Tre before that dirty bitch has you locked up! She ain't worth it!" I heard Kisha yell as she tugged on my arm. "Tre, let her go!" She tried with all of her strength to free Mina from my grasp but it was impossible.

Tyson grabbed me from behind and tried pulling me away from her but I still had her by the hair. I thought about yanking her fuckin' hair so hard that it popped her neck! "Tre let go of her man! I told you not to put your hands on her! Let her go!"

For some reason Ms. Lizzy's voice popped in my head and I could hear her saying. *"Before you do anything stupid think about whether or not you want to make things harder than what they are. Sometimes the best decision we can make is to walk away from it all."*

I reluctantly let go of Mina's hair. As soon as I let go she took off running down the hall to the bedroom and I heard the door slam. "I want that bitch out of my crib yo!" I yelled loud enough for her to hear. "Get yo' shit and get the fuck out bitch! You ain't shit! You gone mistreat my motherfuckin' kids and then have the audacity to brag about that shit! Really bitch? After all that I've done for your funky ass and your daughter? I treat your baby like she's my own and this is how you repay me? I see why Mello was beating yo' ass! You deserved it! It's obvious that a nigga can't be good to you! You don't know how to accept kindness! You are just like most motherfuckas out here, you take that shit as a sign weakness! You got me good though because normally I am the one doing some foul shit to a bitch. This time around though, I guess I met my fuckin' match. You was laughing in my face, fuckin' me and mistreating my kids behind my back every chance you got while I was helping to take care of yours! Yeah you got me good. Made me look like a pure motherfuckin fool!"

"Tre calm down." Kisha told me. "She's not going to come out of that room with you acting like that. You need to calm down and go back there and make sure she ain't calling the cops on your ass!"

The mention of the cops only infuriated me even more. "I wouldn't give a flying fuck who she calls!" I snatched away from Tyson and charged down the hallway towards the bedroom door. I tried to open it but it was locked. I banged on the door with my fists. "Open this damn door! Are you in there calling the cops bitch? Huh? Call them! You can use my gotdamn phone to call them if you want and I will whoop your motherfuckin ass again when they get here!" I yelled through the door.

"I'm not calling the police." Mina sobbed loudly. "I just want to leave...please just let me go. I promise I won't call the police."

"Bitch, you can leave! Ain't nobody holding you hostage! I want your ass to go!"

"You are going to hit me again if I open the door." She accused and to be perfectly honest she was right. I had every intention of knocking fire from her ass no sooner than she cracked that door open. I was beyond pissed, not just at her but also at myself for trusting her.

"Tre, man come away from the door and let her get her shit and leave." Tyson told me. "Come on let's go outside and get some air."

"Hurry up and get your shit and get the fuck out of my house before I change my mind about not whooping your ass again." I yelled through the door. "You've got ten minutes to gather everything that you have here and kick rocks!" With that being said I followed Tyson outside onto the porch. When we got out there I took my cigarettes out of my pocket and lit one up. I took a long pull and inhaled the smoke into my lungs. With the way that I was feeling. I needed something much stronger than a cigarette. I began pacing back and forth shaking my head. I'd really fucked up this time and I didn't have anyone to blame but myself.

Kisha came outside onto the porch. "I'm about to go." She told me and then turned to look at Tyson. "Make sure that he doesn't put his hands on that girl and end up in jail. I have to get home and put my children to bed. I don't want to get a phone call saying that he's locked up."

"You won't." Tyson assured her. "I got him."

"Alright now, if he gets into trouble I am coming for you." She laughed as she walked down the steps.

No matter how fucked up I'd treated her throughout the years, when push came to shove, she'd always had my back. Niggas never realize how good they have it until what they had is gone. "Kisha..." I called after her.

She stopped walking and turned around. "Yes."

"Thank you. I appreciate you letting me know what the deal was. If I'd listened to you from the start none of this would ever have happened."

She shrugged her shoulder. "Yeah, I guess it

wouldn't have but it is what it is now. Good night."

She turned and started walking again. "Hey Kisha..."

She looked back but this time she didn't bother to stop walking. "I already know Tre, you're sorry. You always are." She reached her car, got inside and left.

"I fucked up, Tyson." I told the only friend that I had left. "I really fucked up."

"Man don't be so hard on yourself. We all make mistakes. That's what life is all about, living and learning."

"Yeah, you're right but it's like my ass don't ever learn. Kisha tried her best to warn me about that bitch in there." I pointed towards the house referring to Mina who was still inside. "I wouldn't listen, now look. Then look at how I treated Lala." The thought of how I'd treated Lala nearly caused me to breakdown and cry. Images of the terrified look in her eyes that night when I'd drawn the gun on her after finding out about Reggie played in my mind and it broke my heart. What kind of nigga does that to his own babymama? At that moment, I realized just how fucked up I really was and the things that Ms. Lizzy had said earlier started to make more sense. I couldn't help but get back bad energy because that was all I ever put out. That shit that I'd done to Lala was downright unforgivable. Especially now after finding out the type of bitch that Mina was and realizing that I'd done the same exact thing as she had. I'd left my children with someone, whom I trusted. I ran my hand over my face and pulled on the hair beneath my chin. "I've got to call Lala and apologize. I know that it probably won't make too much of a difference but I have to call her anyways."

"She knows that you were upset when you said and did the things that you did. Everybody who knows you, knows how you are when it comes down to your children so I am sure that she will accept your apology." I think that he was only trying to make me feel better but I was hoping that he was right. "I wouldn't tell her about what ol' girl did though. That right there will only make shit worse before it gets better...believe that. I can already see how that will turn out. Lala ain't going to stop until she beats the brakes off of Mina. You saw all of the blood on the floor at her crib from how she fucked ol' boy up for touching Lil' Mama. I can tell she don't play when it comes down to them babies either. She may have made a fucked up decision by leaving them with dude but she wore his ass out for fucking with her baby."

"Yeah...she did." I let out a sigh and looked out across the yard. I heard the door open and looked backed. Mina walked slowly out onto the porch sniffling, carrying a bag on each shoulder and an armful of clothes. She didn't say anything as she crept past us and made her way down the steps. "Where is my key?" I asked causing her to jump.

She stopped walking and looked up at me on the porch. "I left it on the dresser in the room."

"It better be up there too."

"It is." She started to walk off but then stopped again. "Tre…I'm sorry. I wasn't trying to hurt them, I swear."

"Bitch kick rocks before I fuck you up out here!"

She turned back around and rushed to her car. I stood there and watched her back out of the driveway before walking back into the house. I went into the kitchen, opened the cabinet beneath the sink and took out the half bottle of Paul Mason that I had under there. I sat it on the counter and took down a glass from the cabinet. I pour myself a nice drink and stood there next to the counter sipping it and staring off into space thinking.

Tyson walked into the kitchen a few minutes later. "You good?"

"Nah man." I answered truthfully, tears filling my eyes. "But I plan to drink until I am."

"Mind if I join you?"

"Grab a glass out of the cabinet."

Lala

My mama, Nisey, and I were seated in the living room talking and watching the girls play on the floor.

"I have really enjoyed you girls this week." My mama told us patting me on my leg. "I can't even sit here and lie. I am going to miss the devil out of y'all when you go back. I'm going to miss my grandbabies too." She looked over at me. "I sure wish you would consider moving back down here so that I could be closer to them and you."

I looked over at her and smiled because little did she know the thought had crossed my mind quite a few times. I loved having both sets of the girl's grandparents around to help me with them and I kind of missed living in the country too. Minus the drama with Tre and Kisha, I hadn't ever had any problems with anyone in Boykins because I stayed to myself and didn't bother anyone.

"You know mama, I've been doing some thinking and I have to admit that moving back home has crossed my mind a lot after what happened recently with Reggie.

I honestly don't think that I can continue to stay in that house in Danville because every day that I've spent in that house since that bastard touched my baby, when I walk into the living room I see him touching her all over again." I saw Nisey hang her head and shake it from the corner of my eye. I'd shared this with her before we'd left. "Not only that but when I left Boykins, I left for all of the wrong reasons. I left because I was running from a problem that I'd been woman enough to create but not woman enough to face. I left because I was trying to protect a man who I thought cared something for me when truthfully all he ever cared about was himself. I thought that if I left, it would prove my love for him and show him my loyalty to him. All it showed was my weakness for him but that was then and this is now. A lot of things have changed since then, I've learned so many things over the past year. I've learned a lot over the past few weeks. I'm tired of running but I am more tired of chasing...tired of chasing temporary happiness. After all that has happened with Tre and Reggie, I've learned that no man will ever be able to truly make me happy. First I have to be happy with me...me and only me. True happiness comes from within, it's not out there in those streets and when you go out there seeking it and chasing it like I did, you end up with some bullshit just like I did. Tre and Reggie both were my seasonal men, they weren't meant to be in my life forever...only for a season. That's why in both cases things turned out the way that they did. They were both placed in my life to teach me lessons and they did. Very valuable lessons that I will never forget. I should've known that there could never be anything real between Tre and I. Look at how that man came into my life...all wrong. I fought hard though to be the woman that he chose in the end." I smiled through my tears. "It's a good thing he chose Mina though because this woman that sits before you now is too good for him and I know that I deserve better. I was playing the game trying to win a prize when there never was one."

Nisey wiped her face with both of her hands because she had tears meeting beneath her chin. "Awww shoot now, listen at my best friend. This is definitely not the same girl that I first met in the doctor's office. Hell this ain't even the same girl from a month ago."

"Hmph, sometimes it takes something tragic to open up your eyes and make you start to see shit for what it really is Nisey."

"Amen to that!"

My mama leaned over and wrapped her arms around me giving me a big hug. "I am so proud of you baby. You're finally growing up."

"Me too." Nisey added. "Now let's get back to you thinking about moving back down here and leaving me."

"I was honestly hoping that you would come with me." I looked over at her. "I mean, what's really in Danville for you?"

"Are you serious? You want me to pick up and

move down here to the country in all these sticks with you? Girl, y'all don't even have stores." She teased.

"Whatever. Don't try and joke my hometown." I laughed. "You said that you really don't have a tight relationship with your family and you don't deal with Johnathan's family. My parents have fallen in love with you and I am sure that they will love Evan as well once they meet him. We could be your family."

"You are already my family." She told me. "Let me think about this moving thing for a while and I will let you know something."

"That's cool." I nodded my head. I knew that moving was a big deal and it wasn't a decision that could be made in a couple of minutes. "As for me, I've pretty much made up my mind to move back here."

"That's great!" My mama exclaimed clapping her hands together. "I can't wait to have you back home. I've missed you so much. Oh, I can't wait to tell your daddy! He is going to be ecstatic! How soon are you planning to start moving?"

"As soon as I get back, I am going to start packing." I informed her. "I was looking in the newspaper yesterday morning and saw a three bedroom, one and a half bath house not too far from here. The landlord wasn't asking much for the rent. I've seen the house before. The only bad thing about it is that it's one house over from Mina. That means I will more than likely have to see her and Tre damn near every day."

"No you don't. All you have to do is stay in your house and mind your business. If they come messing with you, let them know that you don't want to be bothered." My mama explained. "Besides you don't have to stay there long. It could just be something temporary to start off with."

"True."

"Call the landlord and ask if you can go by and look at the place. You know, see what it looks like on the inside. If you like what you see, let me and your daddy know and we will pay the first month and the security deposit for you."

"Thanks ma but I can handle the first month and the deposit. You and daddy have done enough."

She waved me off. "Oh hush, talking that nonsense. You are my baby. There is no such thing as ever doing enough. We are going to continue to do for you and those babies until God calls us home." She got up from the sofa. "I am going to go and find your daddy and tell him the good news." She leaned down and gave me a big kiss on my cheek. "You just don't know how happy you done made your mama, honey." She grinned and pranced out of the room.

Nisey made a face at me and threw one of the throw pillows that was on the sofa at me. "You know, I'm not feeling you leaving me!"

"Yeah, I know but I did ask you to come with me!" I tossed the pillow back at her. "Even if you don't come though, that won't come between our friendship. We'll still talk on the phone every day and unless they take the roads up I will definitely be coming to visit you and Evan and I hope that you will come visit me and the girls too."

"Child, you already know that without a doubt." She assured me. "What are you going to do about the situation with Reggie? I mean, don't y'all have to go back to court sometime soon?"

"That's three months away but you best believe I will be there. I refused to allow that motherfucka to get away with what he did to my baby." I rolled my eyes feeling myself becoming heated.

Cuddy Buddy by Tre Songz started to play telling me that Tre was calling. I made a mental note to change his ringtone to something else. I looked around for my phone and realized that it was over on the table next to Nisey.

"Nisey can you toss me my phone please?"

She picked it up, looked at the screen, rolled her eyes and tossed it to me. "We talked his ass up didn't we?"

"Yeah, I guess we did." I said catching the phone. I pressed send to answer and then the phone up to my ear. "Hello."

"Hey, are you busy?"

"Why?" I asked wondering where all of the hostility that he'd been having in his voice when we spoke had gone.

I heard him let out a sigh. "I wanted to talk to you, that's all." There was definitely something different about this Tre that was on the phone with me now. He was a totally different person from the man who'd been ready to beat my ass at his house the week before and the man that I'd talked to a few days ago who hadn't had more than a few words to say to me and they'd basically been 'how are my babies doing' and 'I would like to see my kids before you go back home'.

"About?" I watched as Nisey got up and left the room. I assumed that she was trying to be polite and give me a little privacy while I was on the phone.

"I want to start by apologizing to you for how I've been treating you recently and how I've treated you in the past. I took things too far and I am deeply sorry for that. I let my anger get the best of me and handled things in a fucked up way. I am really sorry for pulling the gun on you that night at your place. I know that I could never say sorry enough to make up for…"

I didn't want to hear anymore. Truthfully the sound of his voice disgusted me. "You know what Tre, you can save your apology for someone who actually wants to hear that bullshit because I don't. For some reason you feel like you can talk to me however you want, treat me like shit and then come back with some lame ass apology and all is good. It ain't going down like that this time. The time when I needed you the most you treated me like I was a fuckin stranger that you didn't know shit about. Instead of you judging me by the mother that I've been to your children since the day that they came into this world, you judge me by one mistake…one bad decision. I will never forget you pointing that gun in my face or that nasty disrespectful comment that you made in front of everyone last week at your house."

"Lala…"

"Lala my ass! I am done with you. If it doesn't concern our daughters then don't call me." I was done playing games with him. "I will be busy concentrating on how to be a fit parent to our daughters so I will have no room for extra bullshit in my life."

"Why are you trippin' like this?" He asked as if he didn't feel like the things that he'd done were that bad. He probably didn't but I really didn't give a damn how he felt. "I don't want things to be like this between us. I understand that you are upset with me and rightfully so but we should sit down, talk and try to get past everything that has happened. We have kids together. We need to try and at least get along for their sake."

I purposely yawned into the phone. "Bye Tre." I hung up my phone and then turned it off. I got up from the sofa and got down on the floor and began playing with my two princesses.

I'd played over and over in my mind for weeks how the conversation with Tre and I would go when we finally did speak and he'd calmed down. Not one time had I imagined that it would go the way that it had but I didn't regret it. I'd said exactly what was on my mind and felt surprisingly relieved...like a huge weight had been lifted off of my shoulders. It was time for a fresh start in my life...a new direction.

Mina

It'd been two weeks since the altercation between Tre and me. I'd been laying low, only going to work and straight back home, afraid that I might run into him in the streets. The anger that I'd seen dancing in his brown eyes that night was similar to the anger that I'd seen dance in Mello's eyes on several occasions. I didn't want any parts of what I knew he was capable of doing to me. I wanted to stay out of his way at least until things blew over some and he calmed down. Also I was pretty sure that he'd told Lala about the entire situation so I was trying to stay out of her way as well, which was proving to be very difficult since she'd become my neighbor. Earlier in the week, I'd seen her, Tre's parents and her parents moving her things into the house down from me. The only thing that separated the two of us was one house. I was more than sure that she'd seen me as well. I knew that she knew where I lived. So far she hadn't bothered me and I prayed that it stayed that way.

I sat in Nelle's bedroom with her and Mia getting ready for her little get-together. I hadn't wanted to come but she'd acted as if she would piss herself if I didn't. I wasn't feeling the thought of being around a lot of people with bruises still visible on my face. I didn't even feel comfortable being around her and Mia.

"Be still." Nelle told me as she tried to apply make-up over my bruises so that no one would see them. I was seated on the chaise that sat at the end of her bed. "The more that I look at these bruises on your face, the more I want to fuck Tre up myself." She spat angrily.

Mia was applying her make-up in the mirror and humming the melody to You and I by Avant and Keke Wyatt. She stopped applying her eyeliner long enough to look at me through the mirror and say. "Yeah he did fuck you up right good." Then she continued what she'd been doing. I could've swore I saw that bitch smirk!

"Child, I ain't worried about that mess." I waved my hand. "He will get what's coming to his as soon enough. He want to go around beating up on women. I wonder if he is going to beat up on Parnell next week when he gets out." I took a sip from the red cup that I'd been holding in my hand. It contained Ciroc and cranberry juice. I definitely wasn't feeling no pain.

"I know that's right because Parnell has made it very clear that Tre's ass is his when he comes home!" Nelle agreed as she applied more make up over the bruise next to my right eye.

I giggled because I'd been throwing a little fuel on the fire since Tre had made the awful mistake of putting his hands on me. He should've listened to Tyson and his babymama and kept his hands to himself. Personally I didn't give a fuck if Parnell beat him until he laid stretched out somewhere lifeless! I'd even went as far as to toss Kisha's name into the mix. I wanted him to get her ass too simply because she had too much mouth and obviously didn't know when to keep it shut and stay in her place. I'd told Parnell how she'd gone around telling people that she was glad Tamika had died. Of course, I'd never heard her say it but he didn't know that. I'd even told him that she'd sat right in the chair in my salon and said it! I hoped that Tre and his babymama got it at the same time. I giggled at the thought and took another sip of my drink.

"What are you giggling about?" Nelle asked.

"Just thinking, that's all." I replied. "So who all is coming to this little shindig?"

"Ummm...not too many people. Just the girls from the shop, their men and a few other people I know." She informed me while smearing some eye shadow on my eyelids. "I think Corey may have invited some of the guys that he work with."

Mia was now humming Secret Lovers by Atlantic Star and messing with her hair. I could tell that something had her in an awfully good mood. I assumed that Ron had given her some good lovin' before they'd left home because she'd even said a few words to me since we'd been at Nelle's and she hadn't been talking to me since the whole falling out about Corey.

"You're in a mighty good mood Mia." I commented feeling like it was okay for me to talk to her since she'd been talking to me.

"She sure is." Nelle agreed. "Ms. Thang has been humming all night long. Ron must've beat that coochie up before they left home!"

Mia played around with her hair for a few more seconds before turning around and looking at us wearing a huge smile. She leaned back against the dresser, the black strapless mini dress that she was wearing hugging her curves. "You two birds need to be more concerned with your own lives instead of everyone else's and then maybe you would be humming too. Instead of always crying the blues."

"Uh-uhh heffa, don't even try and play us like that." Nelle wagged a finger back and forth. "You had better check that 'birds' shit. That's like the second time that you have came off on us like that. You are feeling yourself just a bit too much these days! You might want to come down a couple of notches." She laughed but I could tell that her words held some seriousness in them.

"Damn let me find out that you've become all sensitive like your cousin right there." Mia laughed pointing at me but it sounded forced. I wasn't sure of what to take from the exchange of words that was going on between the two of them. I'd never known the two of them have words about anything but I guess Nelle had gotten a little tired of Mia's funky attitude.

"I'm not being sensitive. I'm just tired of you referring to me as a bird. I don't find it to be cute. You feel me?"

Mia held her hands up in surrender. "Cool cuz, calm down. You got that. I won't joke with you like that anymore. It ain't that serious."

"Cool."

Mia picked her cup up off the dresser. "I'm going to go downstairs. I'll see you two when you get down there. Wouldn't want to piss anybody else off with my jokes." She started towards the door.

"See? There you go." Nelle stopped picking at my hair with her fingers and turned around. Mia stopped walking to listen to what she had to say. "I'm not mad or upset. I'm good. I just didn't find what you said to be funny. This isn't the first time that you made a remark like that and I didn't find it funny the last time that you said it either. However, I let it slide that time but how many times am I supposed to let it slide before I say something to you about it and let you know that I don't like it?"

"Honestly, I don't see what the big deal is Nelle. I've always joked with you about how much you and Mina love to gossip but now that I know it's a problem. I won't do it anymore."

"Fine." Nelle smacked her lips and threw up her hands.

Mia walked back over to her. "Chill out girl! We are good! I'm not mad. I am in too good of a mood to get upset about something as small as this. You and I are good." She assured giving her a hug. "Are you sure that you are not going through something? I mean, you even have tears in your eyes. Why are you so upset?"

I'd noticed the tears too. I started to wonder if she and Corey were still having problems. The thought of it brought a smile to my face, which I tried to hide by putting my cup up to my lips. It was true what people said about misery loving company. Being that my shit was fucked up, I wanted hers to be as well. I sure as hell didn't want her bouncing around me all happy and shit.

Nelle took a seat on the chaise next to me and let out a sigh before wiping her eyes. "It's probably these damn pregnancy hormones." She looked from me to Mia.

"I found out the other day when I went to the doctor that I am about six weeks."

I nearly choked on my drink. "Girl, are you serious?"

"You're what?" Mia asked obviously just as shocked as me. "I thought you claimed that you and Corey have been at each other's throats for the past couple of months or so."

"We have but you know how that goes girl." Nelle snickered. "One minute we fussing and the next we fuckin'."

"Yeah, I sure do know how that go." Mia hugged Nelle. "Congratulations cuz."

"Thank you."

"Yeah congrats girl." I hugged her as well but only not to seem like a hater or look suspicious because I wasn't the least bit happy for her ass. "Are you done with my make-up?"

"Yeah, you're straight." Nelle assured me and then

stood up. "We need to get downstairs because the guests should start arriving at any moment."

"Alrighty then..let's go." Mia said and we all headed for the door.

The party turned out to be better than I'd assumed and more people than I'd expected showed up. I'd spent most of the night talking to and dancing with one of Corey's coworkers. He was a real cutie and seemed to be cool but he wasn't my type at all. His conversation was extremely boring. I found myself drinking to tune him out. I could tell that he was really feeling me and I didn't want to hurt his feelings so I sat through hours of him talking about random stuff that didn't spark my interest in the least. By the end of the night I was so fucked up I could barely walk.

"Mina, I hope that you don't think you are driving nowhere." Nelle said to me as I sat on her sofa with my shoes in my hand. I'd taken them off because they'd began to hurt my feet. "You may as well go ahead upstairs and get in that guest bed."

"I'm good." I assured her slurring my words. "I'm going home and get in my bed."

"Girl, the only bed that you are going to see tonight is the one in the guestroom." She put her hand on her hip. "I'm not going to fuss with you about it either."

"Nelle, I'm fine." I tried to convince her but she wasn't buying it.

"Mina come on here and let me help you upstairs." I stood to my feet and she grabbed my arm wrapped it around her shoulder. "Lean on me." We started up the stairs while Corey showed the rest of the guests out. Mia and Ron had left early because Mia was complaining that her head hurt.

When we got upstairs, Nelle turned the light on in the room for me and led me to the bed. She was treating me like I was stupid instead of drunk.

"I am going to go and find you something to sleep in. I'll be right back." She said and left the room. While she was gone. I stripped out of the dress that I'd been wearing and threw it over on the dresser. I stretched out across the bed in my bra and panties, not bothering to wait for her to come back. First I laid on my back but the room was spinning so bad that I rolled over on my stomach and closed my eyes. In no time, I drifted off to sleep.

A few hours later, I woke up to a pitch black room needing to empty my bladder. I sat up and had to take a few seconds to figure out exactly where I was. I was still feeling the effects of all of the Ciroc that I'd consumed earlier. I got up and staggered out into the hallway, still in nothing but my bra and panties. Nelle had little a nightlight plugged up in the hallway so it wasn't completely dark like in the room. I made my way to the bathroom not bothering to turn on the light or close the door. I sat there in the dark for several minutes trying to get myself together. My head felt slightly woozy. After a while, I stood up, wiped myself and flushed the stool.

As I was leaving out of the bathroom, I heard the door to Nelle and Corey's room open and then close. I started back down the hall to the guestroom, trying to make it before whoever it was saw me because I didn't have on any clothes. I'd made it almost to the door when I bumped directly into Corey wearing nothing but a pair of boxers.

"Oh shit!" He said obviously startled. "My bad Mina."

"Nah, my bad." My eyes roamed over his muscular chest and then down to the boxers that he was wearing. I wanted to see what was in them more than anything in the world.

"Excuse me." He told me and tried to walk past me but I stepped in his path. I may have still been a little tipsy but I wasn't so tipsy that I wasn't well aware of what was standing in front of me. I finally had my opportunity to make my move and even though Nelle was only a few feet away in the bedroom down the hall, I wasn't about to let it slip through my fingers.

I reached out and touched Corey's naked chest, slowly dragging my fingers down further and across his abs. "Damn you are one sexy ass motherfucka." I whispered. "I want you so bad. I find myself watching you and daydreaming about you all the time."

He moved my hand. "Have you lost your damn mind?" He snapped in a hushed tone. "Nelle is right down the hall."

"I know that, we could be really quiet." I tugged on his arm trying to pull him into the bedroom. "Come on, she doesn't have to know. I believe that you want to too."

"Nah, I'm good." He jerked his arm away and shoved me back off of him causing me to stumble back into the wall. Making a light thud. "You are trippin'. I don't know what type of games you are playing but I don't want no parts of that shit!"

Feeling embarrassed, I snapped being careful to keep my voice down. "It ain't that serious damn!"

"It is that serious, my wife is right down the hall…"

"No your wife is right here!" Nelle stood in the middle of the hallway. She flipped on the light switch and walked closer to Corey and me. The pissed expression on her face told me that shit was about to get ugly. She eyed both of us suspiciously. "Does anyone want to tell me what the fuck is going on out here?"

"Ain't shit going on." Corey didn't hesitate to answer. "I was on my way to the bathroom."

"Where in the fuck are your clothes?" She yelled getting up in his face pointing her finger. I took a few steps back.

"They're in the room because I'd forgotten that she was here!"

"Okay so why are you and her out here? And why did I walk up on you telling her that your wife was right down the hall?" She questioned. "Somebody need to tell me what in the fuck was going on out here before I got up!" She looked over at me. "Mina open up your motherfuckin' mouth! You was talking a few minutes ago. What's wrong now? Cat's got your tongue?"

"No, I was on my way back from the bathroom and I bumped into Corey. I asked him where you were and that's when he said my wife is right down the hallway."

Nelle started to laugh, which confused me but not for long. Without warning she slapped the shit out of me and started raining blows in my face and head. "Bitch, I warned you not to ever cross me! You are telling a gotdamn lie! It's worse enough that you would stoop so low as to try and fuck my husband in my house but then you gone lie to my face on top of that." She yelled as she continued to swing on me. I tried to fight back but I was no match at all for her. I was glad when Corey pulled her off of me.

"Chill Nelle, remember you're pregnant!" He told her as he restrained her.

"When Corey got out of the bed, I woke up. I was thirsty so I put on some clothes and came to get some water. You was so busy trying to fuck my husband that you didn't hear me coming. I heard your triflin' ass though, talkin' about 'she doesn't have to know'!" She yelled out of breath, her chest heaving up and down and tears streaming down her face. "You ain't shit! I swear, I have no idea what happened to you but you have turned out to be a very fucked up individual! From this day forward, I don't have shit else for you to do. I am done with you, period point blank! I should've been stopped fucking with you, like everybody else! But no, I tried to be nice and give you the benefit of the doubt. Go and get your clothes and get the fuck out of my house!"

"Nelle it wasn't like you think." That was all I could think to say.

"Just get your stuff and leave." Corey told me still holding onto Nelle.

I went into the bedroom, put back on my dress, and slipped on my shoes. When I was done I went back out into the hallway, Nelle was leaning against the wall and Corey was standing next to her.

"Nelle..."

She closed her eyes biting on her bottom lip. "Girl, if you don't take your ass on somewhere!" She warned. "You don't have shit else to say to me long as you be black. Like I said before, you ain't shit. You gone try something like that in my damn house with me right down the hall? I believe that you have some type of serious mental issues. You might want to get that shit checked out."

I knew there really wasn't anything left to say, to be honest there really wasn't anything that I wanted to say. Things hadn't worked out like I'd wanted them to but I'd tried and I didn't regret it one bit. I'd known that there was a possibility that things wouldn't work in my favor. All I could do was chop it up as a loss and keep it moving.

Kisha

I sat next to Lavar at the Olive Garden enjoying my salad and nearly killing myself laughing. This was our second date and I have to admit that I was really feeling him. So far I'd learned that he was a recently divorced single father of a twelve year old girl and a five year old boy. He had his own place out in Franklin, VA and worked as a supervisor for the paper mill out there. Both of his parents were still living and they lived in Franklin as well. I was very impressed by how he seemed to have his shit together. That made me want to get my shit together even more.

I had managed to get the job at Walmart so I was very happy about that. I'd been working for the past week and I was really enjoying it. They'd given me night shift. I wasn't crazy about staying up all night but I wasn't about to complain either. I had to start somewhere.

Lavar reached over and touched the side of my face. "You have such a beautiful smile." He complimented me, his eyes roaming over my face, causing me to blush and feel a little uneasy at the same time. It'd been a while since I'd had a man compliment me.

"Thank you."

"You're welcome." He told me and then his face took on a serious expression. "I wanted to ask you, what you're looking for as far as a relationship is concerned. I mean, I'm not trying to rush you into anything but I would like to know so that I will know how to carry things with you."

I sat my fork down on my plate and took a sip of my wine before answering. "Well to be honest, I don't know. I can't really say that I am looking for a relationship or that I'm not." I answered truthfully moving my bangs back from my eyes. "I've been through a lot over the past few years as far as relationships are

271

concerned. Right now my main focus is getting my life in order for my boys. I am trying to get to a point in my life where I don't have to depend on anyone else unless I want to, not because I have to. My boys deserve better than what I have been giving them. They deserve stability and a mother who isn't so caught up in a bunch of drama and nonsense that she can't properly take care of her children. I say all of that to say, I like you and I would love to continue getting to know you and if this progresses into something more than a friendship...cool. If not...cool."

"Fair enough, pretty lady." He replied. "Well I would love to continue getting to know you as well but I can't lie, I am praying that it progresses into something more." We both laughed. "You're laughing but I am serious. A man would be a fool to not want to lock you down. You are beautiful and seem to have your head on straight. I like that."

The waitress showed up with our meals and placed

them down in front of us. We both thanked her.

"No problem." She smiled. "Is there anything else that I can get the two of you."

"No thanks, we're good." Lavar replied, answering for the both of us.

"Okay then, call me if you need me." With that she left us alone so that we could enjoy our meals.

Lavar and I were eating and talking about our kids when my phone started to ring. "Excuse me." I told him and then opened my clutch and took out my phone. My mama's name was flashing on the screen. I looked over at Lavar. "It's my mama. I have to take this because it could be something concerning my kids."

"You don't have to explain anything to me." He assured me. "By all means answer it."

I pressed the send button to answer as I rose from the table and walked in the direction of the ladies room. "Hello."

"Hey baby, I'm sorry to interrupt your date but I

just saw something very disturbing at the corner store."

"Huh?" I asked puzzled as I pushed the door to ladies room open and went inside. "Ma what are you talking about?"

"Did you know Parnell was out of jail?"

I laid my clutch on the counter and stood in front of the mirror. I checked my hair and noticed that a few strands of hair were out of place. "I saw something about it on Facebook a few days ago." I told her wondering what Parnell being out of jail had to do with me. "Ma, I'm not trying to be rude but why are you calling me about Parnell. I am trying to enjoy myself not worry about who just came home from jail." I fixed my hair with my fingers and then leaned against the wall.

"Kisha, I know goodness well if I done heard the things that he's said about Tre, you have too. Does Tre know that he's out or that he's here in Boykins? If not he needs to know so that he can watch his back. People are crazy now a days and capable of anything."

I rolled my eyes up in my head becoming agitated. All of this had absolutely nothing to do with me. "Ma, I have no idea what Tre knows. Honestly, I don't care. Tre is a grown man he can take care of himself. Furthermore, I don't believe that Parnell is going to do anything more than talk. Yeah, I've seen little stuff that he's said on Facebook about when he comes home somebody is going to pay for what happened to his sister but I really don't be paying that mess no mind. That's what folks do on Facebook, they front and pop shit but then when you see them in person they are so quiet that you could hear a mouse piss on cotton."

"How in the world did he have access to Facebook if he's locked up?" She inquired acting as if I wasn't on a date at all. "Lord knows I am confused child."

"Ma a lot of inmates have cell phones. People sneak them in to them, sometimes even the CO's."

"Well lord, you sure done told me something. That is really something else, ain't it?"

"Yeah ma, it is." I sighed. "Listen I have to go. I will talk to you when I get home."

"Hold on a second, I still haven't told you what it was that didn't set right with me when I saw that boy at the store."

"Ma, what?" I snapped she was really starting to tap dance on my last nerve. My idea of a good time hadn't included leaving my date at the table alone while I stood in the restroom on the phone gossiping about Parnell and Tre. "Hurry up and say whatever it is that you need to say so that I can go back out into the dining area with my date. That is if he hasn't let me."

"You'd better calm your nerves!" She checked me real quick. "And if he has left you, you do know your way back home don't you?"

"Ma, I didn't drive." I reminded her.

"Girl, that man ain't gone no damn where! Now shut up so that I can tell you what I have to tell you." She snapped. "Parnell was at the store with Mina."

That got my attention. Why in the hell would Mina be with Parnell? How did she know Parnell? Why would the two of them be together three weeks after Tre put her out and only a couple of days after Parnell got out of jail? My gut told me that her ass was up to no good.

"Hello?" Ma spoke into the phone. "Kisha are you still there?"

"Y-yes ma'am, I'm still here." I replied realizing that I'd gotten super quiet.

"Kisha, I don't trust that girl."

"Me either ma." I admitted. "But truthfully whatever they have going on isn't any of my business. Tre might even already know about Mina and Parnell. Knowing her, she is only messing with him to get back at Tre. She probably just wants some attention with her ratchet ass."

I heard her let out a sigh. "Yeah maybe you're right. I sure hope so. I'm going to get off of this phone and let you get back to your date. I'm sorry for bothering you.

It's just that when I saw that mess I had to call somebody. You should've seen the guilty look that she had on her face when she saw me. She even looked a little uneasy."

"I can imagine." I told her. "Okay then, I will see you when I get home. We will talk more then."

"Alright, try to enjoy the rest of your date. I love you."

"I love you too." I disconnected the call, washed my hands and exited the restroom.

When I reached the table a smile cover Lavar's sexy full lips. "Is everything alright, beautiful? I was starting to think that you'd snuck out the backdoor for a minute."

"Nah..." I took my seat back next to him, picked up my fork and began picking at my now cold food. "Everything is fine. One of the boys isn't feeling well." I lied.

"Oh, I'm sorry to hear that." He looked concerned. "Do you want me to take you home? I don't mind. I understand that your baby comes first." He was such a gentleman.

"No it's okay, he just has a stomachache. He will be fine with my mama until I get home."

"Are you sure?"

"Yes, I'm sure."

"Would you like to order something else because I know that is cold now?" He offered pointing to my food.

"No, I'm fine. I don't really have much of an appetite anymore." Truth was now I couldn't stop thinking about Mina and Parnell. Maybe there wasn't anything to their being together other than Mina trying to get back at Tre but when it came to Mina, you could never be too sure. Anyone who would shake and pinch innocent babies who couldn't defend themselves was capable of anything if you asked me. I didn't put nothing past that hoe!

"A penny for your thoughts." Lavar said cutting into my thoughts.

"I'm sorry." I apologized realizing that I was being rude but it wasn't intentional. I kind of regretted answering my phone now because I didn't need to be worried about Tre and his Mina and Parnell issues. Tre was my past, I was trying to work on my future, a future that didn't include him and his drama. He was no longer my problem. Here I was supposed to be on a date getting to know someone new and all I could think about was some mess that didn't have nothing to do with me.

"You don't have to apologize. I understand how it is when something is wrong with one of your children." He explained. "Listen, how about we call it a night and I take you home so that you can take care of little man. Then if he's feeling better, you and I can go to the movies or something tomorrow."

"I guess, I'm not much fun anymore sitting here with my mind somewhere else." I forced a smile. "I apologize again."

"No problem." He waved the waitress over and

asked for the check. After he paid, we left. When we reached my house he walked me to the door. "I had a great time with you tonight Kisha."

"I had a great time with you as well. I'm sorry..." he placed his finger over my lips to silence me.

"Will you please quit apologizing? I am a very understanding man. I knew that you had kids from day one and I also realized that things like this would come up. I honestly would rather you be here with your sick baby than somewhere with me worried to death about him." He leaned over and kissed me on my cheek. "Go on inside and take care of your baby. I will call you before I go to bed to check and see how he is doing. Also so that I can hear your voice before I go to sleep."

"Okay." I blushed and then used my key to let myself inside. Inside, I placed my keys on the coffee table. Ma had fallen asleep in the recliner and left the TV on. I walked over and turned off the TV and fixed the blanket that she had thrown over her legs. I went down the hall, on the way to my room I stopped by the boys room and peeked my head in. They were both fast asleep so I headed on down the hall to my bedroom. I flipped on the light switch, took my heels off at the door and then flopped down on the bed. I opened my clutch and took out my phone and went to my contacts. When I found the name that I was looking for, I pressed it on my touchscreen and waited for the call to connect.

The phone rang several times, I was about to hang up when he picked up. "Hello." Tre's deep voice came through the phone.

"Hey, I hope that I didn't bother you."

"Nah, you straight. I was just laying here watching TV. What's up?"

"Ummm, I called because mama told me that she saw Parnell up at the store earlier. I wanted to know if you knew that he's out or that he's here in Boykins."

Tre burst into laughter. "Kisha, why are you calling me like this nigga is the big bad wolf or something? Fuck him. If he wants to see me, I ain't hard to find. It ain't like I'm hiding or something."

"Tre, I didn't say that he's the big bad wolf or that you are scared. I just want to make sure that you are aware."

"Kisha are you alright?"

"What?"

"I'm just checking. You call me sounding like you are scared to death."

"See? This is what I get for being concerned about your black ass!" I snapped becoming annoyed at how nonchalant he was acting after I'd ended my date early worrying about him.

"Calm down, I didn't mean any harm." He told me. "I appreciate you calling and being concerned but there's no need to be. I ain't thinking about that nigga, for real."

"Okay…I also wanted to warn you that him and Mina were together when ma saw him at the store. I am only telling you this because I don't trust that girl at all. It seems mighty funny that those two are together as soon as he comes home. That leads me to believe that she was dealing with him all along. I know that she knows about the beef between you two. So that tells me that he little ass is up to no good."

Again Tre started laughing. "Damn you over there sounding like a PI. I ain't thinking about that hoe either. I just heard the other day something about her cousin Nelle had to whoop her ass for trying to fuck her husband. So her being with Parnell only means that she is easy and the hoe will fuck anything." He said sounding unmoved by anything that I'd said. "She probably thinks that she is hurting me by fuckin' with him but for real I could care less as long as she stays the fuck away from me, we are good because if she comes within five feet of me I am going to whoop her trifling ass again for what she did to my kids."

"I feel you." That was the only thing that I could think of to say. He'd pretty much expressed to me that he wasn't stressing anything concerning Parnell or Mina. So there was nothing else left to say.

"Again I appreciate you calling me though."

"No problem."

"I heard that you got a new little boyfriend too." He revealed catching me totally off-guard.

"Umm..well...no, I have a new little friend. So whoever you are getting your information from is wrong." I let him know.

"Oh okay, well either way as long as he treats you right and you're happy that's all that matters."

I was really shocked to hear him that. "Thank you, Tre." I smiled.

"No problem. You deserve to be happy and at least this time it ain't one of my boys." He laughed.

I laughed too. "Oh I see you've got jokes tonight."

"Just a few." It felt good to laughed with him for a change because normally we were at each other's throats.

"Well okay then, I am about to call it a night."

"Okay. Don't forget that the boys are getting off the bus here tomorrow."

"Oh, I won't."

"Cool...good night."

"Good night Tre." I disconnected the call feeling a lot better. I went in the bathroom and took a shower. When I was done I put on my night clothes, got in bed and then called Lavar.

Mina

I was in the middle of the bed on all fours with my ass tooted up in the air as Parnell thrust in and out of my ass like his life depended on it. Sweat dripped from him onto my back like raindrops as he grunted like an animal.

"Fuck this ass baby." I told him as I pushed my ass back onto his dick. I hadn't had anal sex since Mello and I were together because Tre wasn't into it. I'd tried to get him to try it a few times but he always popped an attitude like I was asking him to do something that questioned his manhood. I loved anal sex so I felt like I was in heaven with each thrust. "Oooh...yes...just like that." I moaned playing in my wet pussy. "You are going to make me cum daddy." I looked back at him. He had his eyes squeezed tightly together biting down on his bottom lip. His chubby face jiggled each time that he plunged into me. "Fuck this ass harder baby."

"Oooh shit!!!" He growled his face contorting into a scary mask as he pumped faster. I felt his organ grow inside of me and knew that he was almost at his climax. That turned me on even more causing my juices to squirt out onto my fingers. I flicked my fingers back and forth over my clit at a rapid pace and within seconds I was cumming and so was he. He continued to pump in and out of my ass until he'd released every bit of his semen inside of my ass.

I collapsed on the bed face down and he collapsed next to me. This had been our third fuck-session that morning. He was definitely the best lover that I'd ever had, even better than Tre and I hadn't thought that it could get any better, even without the anal sex Tre's sex game had been on point.

"So what are your plans for today?" I turned onto my side, propping my head up on my hand and looking over at Parnell.

"I am going to run over and holla at my mama for a little while. Then probably go by my boy Lamont's crib and see what he's talking about." He told me reaching over and palming my ass beneath the covers. "I haven't really had a chance holla at anyone since I've been home because I have been too busy all up in this good shit that you got. That asshole of yours ain't no joke girl."

"I know." I smiled rubbing his round belly. "I don't have anything to do today so I don't mind you using the car."

"Are you sure? Because my mama already said that she would come and pick me up and that I could use her car."

"I'm sure, you can use my car." I heard light tapping at the door followed by Simya calling my name. I rolled my eyes up in my head and let out a frustrated breath. "Simya go in the living room and watch TV until I come in there." I yelled not bothering to get up from where I was on the bed. She knocked again. I sat up slinging the covers back, I grabbed my robe and put it on. As I stomped towards the door, I could feel Parnell's semen dripping from my ass and running down my legs. When I reached the door, I snatched it opened and looked down at my daughter standing there with her sippy cup in her hand.

She smiled up at me. "Cereal mommy."

"Girl, didn't I tell you to go in the living room and watch TV until I come in there?"

"Mina, she's only two years old. How can you expect her to go in the living room and watch TV all by herself?" Parnell asked from where he was lying on the bed.

I looked back at him. "Because she's not slow. She knows what go and watch TV means."

"She may know what it means but I'm sure she doesn't want to sit in there alone."

I didn't bother responding. Instead, I grabbed

Simya by her hand and led her into the living room. I sat her on the sofa while I went into the kitchen and got her highchair and the box of cereal. I placed her chair in front of the TV, put her in it and then poured some cereal on it for her. I turned Dora on and went back into the kitchen to fill her sippy cup with milk. By the time that I walked back into the living room Parnell was entering the room fully dressed with my car keys in his hands.

"I'm about to roll out. I'll hit you up a little bit later on."

I looked at him wondering if he'd forgotten that the two of us had just got through fucking because there was no way in hell that he'd taken a bath that damn quickly. "Aren't you forgetting something?" I asked with my face screwed up.

"What?" He looked puzzled.

"Aren't you going to take a bath?"

He started laughing. "Girl, I just washed up in the sink."

"Oh…" I replied eyeing him skeptically because I didn't smell a hint of soap on him. He turned and started outside and I followed him. "Be careful."

"No doubt." He replied.

I heard a bunch of commotion next door and both of us turned to see what was going on. It was Lala and the girl that had come to Tre's house with her, jumping up and down in the yard hugging.

"Damn, they sure are happy about something." Parnell commented as he got inside the car.

"It ain't no telling, the fat one is Tre's silly ass babymama."

"That ain't Kisha." He replied staring at Lala. "I remember Kisha being much lighter than that and a lot slimmer."

"Nah that's the girl that he cheated on Kisha with. She has two twin girls by him." I informed him.

"Oh…well I hope she has a black dress in her closet because no sooner than I catch that nigga like I want to, it's over for his ass and that's my good word."

"Stop talking like that. He isn't worth you going to prison for. I can understand you whooping his ass but killing him isn't going to bring your sister back."

"You're right but there ain't no way in hell that motherfucka is going to be walking around breathing and she's not!" I noticed that his whole demeanor had changed so I decided to try and defuse the situation.

I looked around and saw that Lala and her nosey ass friend were looking in our direction. "Baby calm down." I told him.

"I am calm." He snapped slamming the car door and starting the ignition. "I'll hit you later." He put the car in reverse and backed out of the yard. I watched until he got down the road and then went back inside the house.

When I walked back inside Simya was still watching TV so I went down the hall to the bathroom to take a bath. No sooner than I undressed and stepped inside the shower underneath the water, I heard Simya start to cry. "Man damn it! Her ass is going back to mama's house! I can't deal with all of this damn crying." I huffed as I squeezed some body wash onto my bath sponge and began washing myself. A few seconds later the crying stopped. "Thank goodness." I took my time and finished taking my bath and then turned off the water. I stepped out of the shower, dried off and wrapped the towel around myself. I opened the bathroom door and walked down the hall to go check on Simya. As I got closer to the living room, I could hear her giggling and squealing. I walked into the living room and nearly fainted when I saw what was making her giggle.

Mello was sitting on the sofa holding and tickling her. He looked up when I walked into the room. "Hey Mina." I wanted to speak but I couldn't and I wanted to run but I couldn't do that either. I was paralyzed with fear. "You don't look too happy to see me. To be completely honest, you look like you've seen a ghost." He laughed and Simya giggled too. "Mama's face does look funny doesn't it?" He asked Simya and tickled her again before looking back up at me. "You know if you would answer your phone then you would've known that I was coming but I guess you've been too busy whoring and letting niggas fuck you in your ass to take any calls."

"How did you get in here?" I asked my voice trembling.

"Well, I was going to pick the lock but you were so mesmerized by your little boyfriend that you forgot to lock the door when you came back inside."

I cursed myself in my head for leaving the door unlocked but then realized that it really hadn't made much of a difference because he still would've come in anyways. "What do you want?" I asked. "You know that I have a restraining order against you, right?"

He got up, placed Simya on the sofa and walked slowly towards me. I began backing up until I backed into the wall and couldn't back any further. "I came to let you know that you have twenty-four hours to get that nigga up out of here. If he isn't gone by tomorrow this time…well…you'll see what happens. Or should I say that the news will be covering what happened. You can think that I am bullshitting if you want but you will be sorry." He threatened. "I hope you've had all of the fun that you've wanted because daddy is home and I am about to get shit back in order."

Tears streams down my cheeks as I shook my head from side to side. "No…I don't want…"

He grabbed me by my throat and squeezed cutting off my sentence along with my air supply. "Plain and simple, if you don't want to be with me and be a family then you sure as hell ain't gone have the next nigga raising my daughter." He let go of my throat and walked back over to the sofa and kissed Simya on her cheek. "Daddy will see you later." He told her and then looked back at me. "Don't forget what I told you…twenty-four hours." He started towards the door but then stopped. "Oh yeah and you can feel free to call the cops if you want. I bet I will get to you before they get to me." He laughed and then walked out the front door.

Lala

"I am so glad that you decided to move down here with me." I told Nisey as we sat at the kitchen table sipping coffee. She'd arrived at my house the day before and announced that she'd made up her mind to move with me.

"Yeah, I figured that a change might be good for me." She admitted as she adjusted her robe. "My mama seemed a little upset to see Evan go but I promised her that I would bring him to visit her as often as I could."

"That's good. Did you get a chance to talk to Johnathan's mother?"

"Nah..." She shook her head. "They don't give a

damn about me moving away with Evan. It's not like they have anything to do with him anyways."

"I feel you. That's just sad because regardless of how they feel about you, he is still their blood."

"Hmmm try telling that to them fools."

I heard one of the girls start to cry and got up from the table. "I will be right back." I rushed down the hall to the girl's room. Lola was standing up in her crib crying. When she looked up and saw me she quieted right down. "You had better hush up that fuss little girl." I smiled at her as I let down the rail and took her out giving her a kiss on her chubby little cheek. I felt her pamper and saw that she was wet so I placed her on the changing table and changed her. When I was done I took her back down the hall with me. "Are you going to show Aunt Nisey that you can walk now?" I asked placing her on the floor.

"Come here Lola." Nisey called to her. She stood there at first looking from me to Nisey and then walked right into Nisey's arms. "Awwww look at Auntie's big girl!"

I got the cereal down from the cabinet, took Lola from Nisey and placed her in her highchair and poured her some cereal on it. Then I filled her cup with juice and sat it next to her before taking my seat back at the table.

"So is your babydaddy still going to watch the kids for us tonight so that we can get out of the house for a little while?"

"Yes ma'am, I texted him this morning and asked him again. He texted back and told me that he would."

"He does know that Evan is coming too, right?"

"Yes Nisey." I laughed "He knows."

"I'm just making sure."

"Well I am going to go and put on some clothes so that I can go by Tre's parent's house. His mama wants to see the girls and she's been complaining about me not coming to visit her." I said rising from the table. "Are you going to go over there with me?"

"Nah, Evan and I are going to stay here while you

go and visit your in-laws." She teased.

"You're not funny." I left out of the kitchen and went to take my bath and get dressed.

When I was done, I gave both girls a bath and put their clothes on. Then Nisey and I did their hair.

"Thank you so much for your help with the girl's hair." I told her as me and the girl's headed out the door.

"You know I don't mind." She said standing in the door way. "Y'all have fun."

"We will. You just be dressed by the time that I get back. We have to drive to North Carolina to the movies and I want to try and catch the seven o'clock movie so that we won't be too late coming back and picking up the kids."

"I'll be ready." She assured me and then went inside the house and the girls and I headed to Tre's parent's house.

When I pulled up in the yard, I noticed that Kisha was there. "Lord please just let her act civilized." I prayed as I got out of the car and then got the girls out. We walked up to the door and rang the bell. After a few seconds of waiting the door opened and Mr. Jefferson stood on the other side holding it.

"Hey Lala." He greeted me and then reached down and scooped up the girls. "How is papa's two favorite girls?" He asked kissing them both. He stepped back out of the way and I walked inside.

"Hey Mr. Jefferson." I spoke and then walked into the living room where Mrs. Jefferson, Kisha and the boys were seated. "Hey y'all." I waved. Everyone spoke back including Kisha.

"Put them down honey so that I can see them walk." Mrs. Jefferson told Mr. Jefferson. He did as she said and both girl took off in different directions. Mrs. Jefferson's hands went up to her mouth. "Awwww...ain't that the most precious sight that you've ever seen?"

"I didn't know that they could walk." Quan said holding his arms out for Laila. "Come here Laila." He told her. She looked at him and went the other way."

"She doesn't like you." Shaun laughed.

"Do so!" Quan yelled getting up in Shaun's face.

"Alright you two!" Kisha sat up on the edge of her chair. "Don't y'all even think about starting that foolishness."

Mrs. Jefferson smiled a proud smile. "It sure feels good to have all of my grandbabies here together and you two as well. I wish my bigheaded son was here."

Kisha's phone started to ring. She took it out of her pocket and answered. "Hello...fighting with who...when? Lord have mercy, I tried to tell him that boy was coming for him." She jumped to her feet and started towards the door. "Where is he at now?"

Somehow I knew that it was something dealing with Tre. I could tell by the look on her face. Instinctively, I jumped to my feet too and started out the door behind her. Mr. and Mrs. Jefferson was right behind us.

"What's going on Kisha?" Mrs. Jefferson asked.

Kisha told whoever was on the phone that she was on her way and then hung up. "It's Tre...Skeet said that him and Parnell just got into a fight at the store. He said that it was pretty bad. Tre is hurt but he won't listen to anybody and go to the hospital."

"Lord have mercy that boy is about to worry me to death." Mr. Jefferson said taking off his hat and scratching his head.

"Did Skeet say where Tre is now?" I asked my heart beating fast. Hearing that Tre was hurt had me nervous and feeling like I had when he'd gotten shot. Even though we weren't on the best of terms at the moment it didn't mean that I wanted anything to happen to him. He was still the father of my children.

"Skeet said that he asked Tyson to take him home."

"Oh shit!" I said and dashed for my car. The first thing that crossed my mind was the gun that he'd had with him when he'd came to Danville.

"What is it Lala?" Mrs. Jefferson was at my car

303

window, panic written all over her face. "What's wrong?"

"I have to get to Tre before he does something stupid. He has a gun!" I told her starting the car. "Keep an eye on the girls. I don't have time to talk."

Without warning Kisha opened up my passenger door and jumped in on the other side! "Drive damn it!" She ordered. I put the car in reverse and backed out of the yard.

On the way to Tre's house neither of us said a word. I was too afraid of what we might find once we made it there. *Lord please let Tre be okay.* I prayed silently as I turned onto his street.

"Lord have mercy, I am so damn nervous my entire body is trembling." Kisha spoke for the first time since we'd been in the car. I glanced over at her and saw a tear roll down her cheek. "I know that he's an asshole but I don't know what I'd do if something happened to him."

I reached over and squeeze her hand. "He's going to be alright. I don't think he's hurt that bad if he asked

Tyson to take him home. I am more worried about what might happen if he goes after whoever he got into a fight with, with that gun."

"That's what has me worried!" She admitted wiping her face. "I didn't even know that his crazy ass had a gun."

"Oh yeah...he has one." I said images of him standing with it aimed at my face flashed in my mind. I shook my head in an attempt to shake the images away. It still hurt to think about it, yet here I was going to make sure that he was okay as usual.

I reached Tre's house just in time to see him and Tyson coming out of the house and rushing down the steps. I pulled in the driveway behind Tre's car purposely blocking him in. Kisha and I jumped out of the car at the same time, not bothering to turn off the car or close the doors.

"Lala move that shit out the way!" Tre yelled holding his car door open. Blood was pouring from a gash in his head, his lip was busted and his shirt was half ripped off.

"No she ain't moving nothing!" Kisha answered before I could. "Look at you! You are bleeding bad Tre! You need to take your ass to a doctor!"

"Kisha, I ain't trying to hear that shit right now. Now move the gotdamn car!" He barked. "Fuck the hospital. As a matter of fact the only place I'm going tonight is prison!"

"Boy stop talking crazy! Think about your kids! If you don't want to go to the hospital, don't go but please go back in the house and let that shit go!" I told him. "What are you really solving by going out there in the streets and shooting somebody? Let that shit go Tre!"

"Fuck that!" He pushed me back out of the way. "Both of y'all take your asses home!"

"No, I'm not going anywhere!" I told him not budging. "Why can't you just listen some damn time? Think about your kids. You claim they are the most important things to you. Well act like it right now and take your ass back in the house before someone gets hurt behind a bunch of foolishness!"

"For real Lala, I'm not trying to hear that shit right now! This shit right here ain't got nothing to do with my kids!"

"It has a lot to do with our kids, what good are you to them dead or in prison?"

"Look y'all are getting on my gotdamn nerves! I ain't gone ask y'all no more to take your asses on somewhere..."

"I'm not going no fucking where because you are being stupid!" Kisha was crying again and so was I. "Why can't you just let this shit go before you end up dead Tre? Don't you ever get tired of this bullshit?"

"I wasn't fuckin' with nobody! That nigga snuck up on me and hit me in my gotdamn head with a motherfuckin' bottle!" He roared. He was so close in her face that their noses touched. "Don't ask me to let that shit go! I'm not about to walk around like some hoe-ass nigga looking over my shoulder everywhere I go! Fuck that! I didn't kill his sister! Casper did! I'm sick of that nigga threatening me! We are going to settle this shit today once and for all!"

"So that makes sense to you?" Kisha didn't let up. "What if you end up dead Tre? You ain't the only one with a fuckin gun, you know? What am I supposed to tell your kids when they grow up and want to know what happened to their daddy?"

"I don't know tell'em whatever you want. Now move the hell out of the way!"

"Fine since you don't give a fuck and you are hell bent on going, I'm going too!" She snatched the backdoor of the car opened and hopped inside locking the door.

"Yo Tre, you need to get your babymamas under control man!" Tyson shouted from where he stood on the other side of the car. "We got shit to do!"

"You shut the fuck up!" I snapped frustrated. Here

Kisha and I were trying all we knew how to keep Tre from going out into the streets and doing something stupid. Instead of him thinking logically and telling him to leave the shit alone too, he was encouraging it.

"You shut the fuck up!" I started around the back of the car at him but before I made it halfway. I heard the screeching of tires and Tyson yelling something with a look of terror on his face, I turned and saw what looked to be Mina's car at the end of the road but things progressed so fast from there that I couldn't be sure. All of a sudden my entire body felt as if it was on fire and everything went black after that.

Tre

The next day I lay in hospital with a gunshot wound to the hip and one in my side, still in shock of the events that had taken place the day before. The shit just didn't seem real to me but I knew that it was because it'd been on the news all night long. I'd turned off the TV because I couldn't take seeing it anymore. Every time their pictures showed on the screen it made me sick to my stomach. Again I'd been blessed and my life had been spared. I knew that I should be glad and thanking God but I couldn't because I knew that those bullets should've claimed my life and not theirs. Tears ran from my eyes as I lay there looking out of the window feeling a surge of mixed emotions. I felt bad about Tyson but the thought of Lala being gone damn near took my breath away. I couldn't hold it in any longer, I broke down and cried like I'd never cried before. After all of the fucked up things that I'd did to her, she'd still been there trying to keep me from doing something stupid or losing my life and it had ended up costing her hers. I knew that the guilt of her death would forever haunt me and rightfully so because she would've never been there if it wasn't for me.

"Son it's going to be alright." My mama got up from the seat that she'd been sitting in next to my bed. She sat next to me on the bed and wrapped her arms around me, lying my head on her chest. "It's going to be alright." She rocked me back and forth. I felt her tears wetting my face and mixing with mines. This was a sad day for all of us. I heard the door open but I didn't bother to look and see who it was.

"Hey, how is he doing?" I heard Kisha ask my mama.

"Not too good." Ma answered her. "Who is your friend?"

"This is Lavar, Mrs. Jefferson. Lavar, this is Mrs. Jefferson, my children's grandmother."

"Hello nice to meet you." I heard a deep baritone voice and turned around to put a face to the voice. "Hey man, sorry for your loss." He told me.

"Thanks man, I'm Tre." I extended my hand.

"I'm Lavar." We shook hands and he stepped back next to Kisha and put his arm around her shoulder in a comforting manner.

"Well, they believe that they've found Parnell." Kisha blurted, her eyes were swollen from crying and she looked exhausted.

I sat up. "What do you mean, they believe that they've found Parnell?" I asked confused.

"Mina's house burned down this morning. All the way down to the ground." She revealed her face reflecting grief. "On the news they say that they've found the remains of several victims and it could take a while for them to identify all of them. The reason why they think Parnell was one of the victims is because Mina's car was parked in the garage and that's the car that he was driving yesterday when..." She didn't finish her sentence. She hung her head shaking it from side to side and I saw tears start to fall. "Lord knows, I pray that her daughter wasn't inside. That's all that I have been thinking about since I heard. Even though I didn't care for Mina, I hate it for her too. No one deserves to lose their life that way."

I hated it for Mina and her daughter too but as for Parnell I couldn't help but find some comfort in knowing that he'd died in such a fucked up way. To me he deserved it and I didn't feel an ounce of remorse for him or any of the other niggas who were with him and had taken part in Lala's and Tyson's murder. The only thing that would've made it better is if I could've personally watched those motherfuckas burn.

"This is why, I want to change and get my life together." Kisha spoke tearing me away from my thoughts. "Because of shit like this. Now Lala's babies have to grow up without their mother. That's some sad shit!" She stood up and walked towards the door. She placed her hand on the knob and then looked back at me. "I hope and pray to God that this right here changes you because if it doesn't then there is no hope at all for you."

"Hold up a minute, you are talking like I did this shit! Like, I pulled the trigger."

"You did!" She spat through tears. "You did because we both begged you to leave that dumb shit alone, go back in the house and put the gun away but you wouldn't listen. You were hell bent on going after Parnell. If I hadn't gotten in the backseat when I did then I would be dead too and so would you. The only thing that saved you was that you were leaned over in the backseat trying to get me out of the car so that you could leave." She shook her head and walked out of the room crying. Lavar followed her.

I laid there for a few minutes after they'd the room just staring at the door, one thing playing over and over in my head. *Before you do anything stupid think about whether or not you want to make things harder than what they are. Sometimes the best decision we can make is to walk away from it all.* The words that Ms. Lizzy had told me.

I closed my eyes and images of Lala's beautiful face filled my head. I could see her smiling and those beautiful eyes of hers staring at me. The strange thing was that images I was seeing of her in my mind were of the first day that I'd ever laid eyes on her... If only I could go back to those last few moments before that car had pulled up in front of my house. I would've gladly traded places with her but I couldn't instead I had to live with her blood on my hands for the rest of my life.

A Glance at Crazy In Luv 2...

Corey

"Nelle calm down shawty and repeat that again but slower and a little bit calmer." I was having a hard time making out what she was saying because she was beyond hysterical on the other end of the phone.

"Corey, I just found out that Mina's dead!" She cried. "Oh my God Corey! I know that she did some foul shit to me but she was still my blood. I can't believe that she's gone!"

"What?" I asked not able to believe what I was

hearing. "Man damn, I'm sorry to hear that. Are you sure that she was inside the house?"

"Yes, her car was still parked in the garage and everything. Her mama had Simya, thank goodness." She sobbed. "Corey please come home. I don't want to be by myself and I can't get in contact with Mia."

I let out a sigh. "Alright baby, I'm on my way. Let me go holla at my supervisor and tell him that I have an emergency at home. I'll be there shortly, okay."

"Okay...and Corey drive safe."

"I will baby." I disconnected the call and looked over at Mia, who was stretched out naked lying in bed next to me propped up on her elbow and staring in my face...Crazy In Luv 2 coming soon!!!

Thank You's

First and foremost I would like to thank God for everything. Without him nothing would be possible. I thank him for blessing me with this wonderful gift to be able to write and entertain people with my stories. Secondly, I would like to thank my three beautiful babies, Ny'Ajah, Camari, and AnTeyvion. You three are the reason that I grind so hard and continue to strive for more and to become a better me. I would like to thank my mom, Angela Taylor and my dad, Paul Hill. I am thankful for and appreciate you both. To my grandmothers Ann West and Mable Hill, I love you both and thank you for being there for me whenever I have needed you both. To my sister and my best friend Tinika Taylor, I love you more than life itself. You are my rock, the one person I can depend on when everyone else in this harsh world has turned their backs on me! I treasure every moment that the two of us spend together.

To all of my aunts, uncles and cousins, I love you guys. R.I.P to my uncles Steve and Calvin, I miss you both very much. A special shout out to my uncle Al Kelly, even though we don't get to see each other much anymore because of our hectic schedules, I love you to pieces and thank you so much for the love and support that you have shown me. Thank you to my sister from another mother Denise Mason, I love you girl and appreciate you. Thanks for listening to my constant drama lol even though I already know what you be saying in your head when I be yapping…lmao! To my cousin, Teresa Porter (my late night, early morning riding partner). Thanks for being there for me the times when I have needed you the most to just be a listening ear.

Now I'd like to thank all of the fans who have followed my work! Thank you to each and every one of you who has ever purchased any of my work or just taken time to read an excerpt of mine. I appreciate it. Thank you to Cash who has believed in a sista since day one. I can't begin to express to you how much your friendship and constant advice and support means to me, I love you and will always treasure our friendship.

To all of the wonderful authors who have supported me or just given me advice, thank you. Aaron Bebo, Jason Hooper, Aleta Williams, Authoress Redd, Andrionna Williams, Candice Stevenson. There are a few of you who have been some real riders so I definitely have to shout you out. Kendra Littleton, Brandi McClinton, Novie Cuteyez, Sharon Blount, Skeet the Poet, Karen Patterson, Chyna Blue, Raychelle Williams, Shayna Williams, Judy Richburg, and Shaniqua Townes. Shout to one of the best book clubs BRAB! You guys rock!!! Thank you all so much. If I have forgotten any one I truly apologize. I suck at this lol. Please know that it wasn't intentional.

And A Special Thank You To

#teamsidechic!!!!